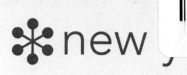new york's
50 best
places to
take
children

By Allan Ishac

4th edition

"Indispensable." — Parents League of New York

universe publishing

First Universe edition published in 2003
By UNIVERSE PUBLISHING
A Division of Rizzoli International Publications, Inc.
300 Park Avenue South
New York, NY 10010
www.rizzoliusa.com

Copyright © 1997, 2001, 2003, 2005, 2009 by Allan Ishac

Designed by Paul Kepple and Jude Buffum @ Headcase Design
Cover illustration by Sujean Rim

2012 2013 / 10 9 8 7 6 5 4 3

Fourth Edition

Printed in the United States of America

ISBN: 978-0-7893-1899-2

Library of Congress Catalog Control Number: 2009902373

Acknowledgments

You wouldn't be holding this book without the help I received from Juliana Kreinik, who applied her formidable research and editing skills so this new edition would be current and readable. Thanks also go to Juliana for creating the day trips section, a useful new feature in this edition. I also want to thank the many parents who sent me entry ideas, especially Elke Deitsch who generously divulged Ella's "secret" list of great locations, and Erick and Jen Johnson who shared Lia's city winners. Also, my gratitude extends to my publisher, Charles Miers, and to my current editor, Claire Gierczak, and all the friendly folks at Universe who, with their continued enthusiasm and support, keep this title alive and readily available for fun-seeking families in New York.

Publisher's Note

Neither Universe nor the author has any interest, financial or personal, in the locations listed in this book. No fees were paid or services rendered in exchange for inclusion on these pages. Please also note that while every effort was made to ensure accuracy at the time of publication, it is always best to check websites and call ahead to confirm that the information is current. New York attractions like the 50 Best also get crowded, particularly on weekends, during holidays and when schools are on vacation. Again, call ahead to check the best times to avoid large groups.

Dedication

To the newest members of my cherished family,
Skyla and Penelope.

contents

20 more great places to take kids (just for the fun of it!)

134 six day trips for foolproof fun

introduction

This is a great time to be a kid in America. We have young children living in the White House again for the first time since Amy Carter cuddled her cat, Misty Malarky Ying Yang, in the family quarters more than 30 years ago.

Of course, the arrival of the two Obama girls in Washington means we're all going to be hearing a lot about Malia's soccer games (good for youth fitness initiatives), Sasha's piano lessons (good for school arts programs), the books that the sisters are reading (good for libraries), and the TV shows they're watching (good for the *Simpsons* . . . just a suggestion, girls). We'll also be watching closely when they walk their new puppy, start a new clothing trend, update their Facebook pages, style their hair differently, share their favorite music, or have a sleep-over party.

Here's the good news: if the nation is focused on the welfare of the First Kids, it will inevitably be focused on the needs of your children, too. The result that we can hope for is more money for public education, improved safety and security for our youngest citizens, increased funding for child-related advocacy programs and aid organizations, and greater respect for children in general. Hurray!

It is also possible that the Malia-and-Sasha phenomenon will lead to a celebration of children as never before. New York City kids and visiting families will get the red carpet treatment wherever they go. Maybe it will inspire the city to redouble its efforts to create wonderful parks, cool playgrounds, safer bikeways, and more child-centric activities and fun events in all of the five boroughs. Who knows—soon these 50 Best Places could be followed by a hundred more.

As you read through, you'll notice that I have not listed hours of operation for places in this book. This is mainly because opening and closing times change quite often. It's wise to call ahead or check websites for up-to-the-minute information. In addition, you'll find a note on the **Ideal Age Group** (covering ages 2 to14), which is based on my observations of children visiting the locations. Since every child is unique, you'll need to be the judge of whether a particular place is appropriate for your child.

For this 4th edition, I've added a handy **Neighborhood Index** (page 139), so that you can easily locate great places from any point in the city. The section entitled **Six Day Trips for Foolproof Fun** (page 134) is also new, offering you a convenient plan for a full day of adventure. Finally, if you've purchased this book looking for unique and unexpected birthday party ideas, you'll be glad to know that most of the locations here can accommodate your guests. Just call well in advance for pricing and particulars.

I'm honored that you've chosen this book as your source for wonderful places to take children. I have tried to write it with a spirit of respect for children, which I hope is in keeping with the uplifting scenes I see coming out of the White House. To watch Michelle and Barack Obama admiring their daughters, showering them with hugs, and nurturing them with parental love has to be good for our national soul. And, ultimately, it inspires hope for the only First Family that really matters . . . yours.

✳ new york's 50 best

50 best

(A to Z)

abracadabra

❄ *Address: 19 West 21st Street, between Fifth and*
   Sixth Avenues
   Phone: 212-627-5194
   Ideal Age Group: 5 to 14
   Admission: Free to browse
   Website: www.abracadabrasuperstore.com

Terror and tickles are served up in equal measure at this enormous ghoul, gag and gift shop, offering one of most thrilling visual experiences in New York. Just keep in mind that terror is the first to greet you at the door with rafter-hanging corpses, puking zombies, leering gargoyles, bloody brides, and a writhing man in an electric chair crowding the vestibule.

It's all in good fun at Abracadabra, and once your kids get past the spooky funeral scene at the entrance, the blood and guts will make way for equally eye-popping but less shocking stuff. Look this way folks and you'll see a life-sized knight on horseback, a stuffed lioness, Han Solo frozen in carbonite, and a 12-foot skeleton dangling from the ceiling. Over here, we have a massive magical wizard with a 10-foot beard, King Tut's sarcophagus, and a bizarre family of aliens. That's just the start.

The Pinzone brothers took over this fun shop in 2007 and have added more wacky stuff, oddball props, amusing costumes, and life-sized stuffed animals, and all are for sale or rent. In fact, the prop managers for *Law & Order* and the MTV network are regular customers here because, well, where else are you going to find a 7-foot tall, blood-stained Abominable Snowman for your show's Himalayan skit?

Abracadabra is also known as Halloween central, and the proof surrounds you. They keep more than twenty thousand kid and adult costumes in stock from life-like gorilla suits and oversized rabbit getups to ornate gladiator armor and 1950s cheerleading uniforms. There might be a major film studio with a costume inventory this vast, but it's not likely. Abracadabra is also the Mecca for professional theatrical make-up (I loved the ghoulish scars and oozing wounds), plus wigs in every style and color, dramatic masks, and the most hilarious assortment of rotting yellow hillbilly teeth I've even seen.

While the Pinzones are especially fond of their horror props, there are also plenty of friendly toys, puppets, cowboy hats, and other harmless gags to distract more sensitive children from any nearby decapitations. Of course, the average nine-year-old is going to see the snotty nose gag, the fart spray, and the awesome belch powder, and demand an Abracadabra party bag.

new york's 50 best places to take children

Cool Kid's Corner

With a name like Abracadabra, you're probably wondering where to find the magic? It's right here every day, and it's free. The Pinzones keep a professional magician on staff at all times, and you can ask for a private magic show whenever you visit. Now all you have to do is tear yourself away from the giant orangutan, the stuffed Great White Shark, the bizarre Mardi Gras masks, and the rest of the wall-to-wall attractions that make this place so much fun. How big are your eyeballs? They'd better be very big, because at Abracadabra they won't get a moment's rest.

alice in wonderland sculpture

❖ *Address: Central Park near Fifth Avenue and 74th Street*
Ideal Age Group: 2 to 7
Admission: Free
Website: www.centralparknyc.org

I have a friend who's a child development expert. She tells me that once children have been immersed in a world of quick-cut TV cartoons, action-packed video games, and high-speed digital gadgetry, it's very difficult for them to settle down and enjoy the slower, simpler pleasures of life. While that may be true, you certainly wouldn't know it from a visit to the Alice in Wonderland Sculpture in Central Park.

There are no bells or whistles here, no keyboards or joysticks, no flashing lights or microprocessors, not a flicker of fast-paced movement anywhere. It's about as low tech as you can get. Yet, every day, children exit the information highway to make an enthusiastic pit stop at this delightful storybook sculpture—a virtual city landmark that's been drawing kids like a big bronze magnet for fifty years (2009 is its golden anniversary).

To be perfectly honest, I never much liked Lewis Carroll's *Alice in Wonderland* story as a child—too convoluted and weird for me. But you don't have to appreciate the book to enjoy this sun-swept, south-facing sculpture. Just one glimpse at the ten-foot tall Alice astride her giant toadstool—surrounded by the zany, fictional characters from Wonderland—and every fiber of a child's body shouts "Climb!" I've even seen two-year-olds bound out of their strollers to explore the underworld of Alice's mushroom forest.

Sculpted by Jose DeCreeft in 1959, this memorial was a gift from philanthropist George Delacorte to his wife, Margarita, who according to the bronze dedication plaque, "loved all children." If there's any question that all children love this sculpture, just examine handholds like the Cheshire Cat's ears, the mouse's tail, the March Hare's pocket watch, and Alice's extended right arm—all burnished to a bright bronze shine by the sweat and oil from thousands of eager little hands.

I must confess, the temptation to climb onto Alice's broad lap and rest my head against her shoulder overcame me. A few four-year-olds stared and wondered why—but Alice didn't seem to care.

A cautionary note to parents: A favorite challenge for children older than seven seems to be a fast ascent to the top of Alice's head, where they hold onto her hair bows like reins. This looks unnecessarily risky to me, especially since the sculpture's base lacks that soft fall, rubbery surface appearing in so many outdoor playgrounds these days. Keep a casual eye on kids of all ages.

If you have an extra hour during spring or summer, walk a few steps south to **Kerbs Conservatory** and rent a model boat from the sailboat guy (page 51). It's another simple pleasure that kids love . . . and that puts my friend's child development theories to the test.

Cool Kid's Corner

Here's a fun game for children under six: See if you can find the lizard under the big toadstool, the caterpillar on the old tree, the squirrel popping out of his tree hole, the little snail, and the Style 10/6 card in the Mad Hatter's top hat.

amc loews imax theatre

Address: 1998 Broadway at 68th Street
Phone: 212-336-5020
Ideal Age Group: 5 to 14
Admission: $16.50 adults / $13 children
Website: www.enjoytheshow.com

new york's 50 best places to take children

I am obsessed with movies, and will watch them anytime and anywhere that I can—with a group of friends in the theater, home alone sprawled in front of the TV, even on my laptop. Movies transport me to other identities (as in "Bond, James Bond"), and nothing makes those journeys more magical or thrilling than watching them unfold on the biggest screen possible. At the AMC Loews Theatre near Lincoln Center, the IMAX definition of "big" borders on the ridiculous.

At 81 feet high by 101 feet wide, the IMAX movie screen here is the largest in the northern hemisphere and one of the two largest on the planet. And while your eyes are astonished, your ears will be astounded by a 12,000-watt surround-sound system that makes the on-screen action seem even more spectacular. You haven't seen anything until you've watched a giant Harry Potter soar past on his Firebolt, an oversized Spiderman swinging between NYC skyscrapers, or the Dark Knight racing on his high-powered, two-wheeled Batpod through the streets of Gotham.

For the ultimate movie-going experience, bring your kids here when there's a 3-D movie on the IMAX menu. Suddenly the picture is not only big (stampeding buffalos as big as bulldozers, frolicking fish the size of freighters), it's also spilling off the screen into your lap.

The 3-D fun begins when you take the escalator past the 75-foot, Hollywood history mural, up to the 600-seat theater (very comfy seats) and are handed your special 3-D glasses.

IMAX is the world's largest film format (ten times larger than standard 35mm), which enables the theater to project that monstrous image the size of an eight-story building. Add to that IMAX's advanced, electronic 3-D technology, and suddenly the movie action surrounds you, zips past your head, hovers at the tip of your nose, and sneaks up behind you. Invariably, lots of little hands reach out to snatch passing 3-D images from the air (okay, I did it, too).

The IMAX theater at AMC Loews was one of the first in the nation to feature full-length classics released in 3-D format, like *Beauty and the Beast* and *Fantasia*, as well as the more recent hits *The Polar Express*, *Robots*, and *Charlie and the Chocolate Factory*. They also have fascinating environmental and discovery films like *Ghosts of the Abyss*, *Aliens of the Deep*, and *Wild Safari 3-D*. While 95 percent of the IMAX film offerings are G-rated, they also have spectacular concert films for teens and adults.

Cool Kid's Corner

Besides showing BIG screen IMAX movies, this cinema complex is also the site of BIG movie premieres with BIG stars. Tom Hanks was here for *The Polar Express* opening years ago and James Cameron made an appearance for *Aliens of the Deep*. Once, my nephew Zachary was up from Florida, when we saw Eddie Murphy pull up in a stretch limo for a movie opening here. Eddie walked right up to my nephew, winked, and shook his hand. Zach still tells his friends it was the coolest thing that ever happened to him in New York.

american girl place

❊ *Address: 609 Fifth Avenue at 49th Street*
Phone: 877-AG-PLACE
Ideal Age Group: Girls 3 to 12
Admission: Free to store
Website: www.americangirl.com

Come within a four-block radius of Fifth Avenue and 49th Street and you'll see dozens of young girls walking with bright red shopping bags. Inside those bags are outfits for Julie, hats for Josefina, shoes for Samantha, accessories for Kirsten and, of course, books about Kit—the Depression-era character whose plucky adventures were brought to life by actress Abigail Breslin in the popular 2008 film, *Kit Kittredge: An American Girl*.

The beautifully designed American Girl Place theme store is at the heart of this doll phenomenon, as important to girls today as Barbie was to their counterparts four decades ago. I must admit that I hesitated outside the revolving entrance doors as I waited for a gaggle of giggling girls—each holding her own freshly coifed American Girl doll—to pass through. My balk was understandable . . . I'm male. And other than a few hapless-looking dads milling about, we are definitely in the minority here.

The funny thing is that I had a wonderful time at American Girl Place, and three hours later, I understood why more than eleven million girls have a Kit or a Kaya, an Addy or a Molly in their lives. The historical roots and compelling stories of each doll are certainly factors. Their differing ethnicities and cultural backgrounds also allow young girls to choose dolls that share their identities. But I think the appeal is more fundamental than that—with their open and friendly faces, American Girl dolls are easy to like.

Another popular attraction within the store is the American Girl Café where they have mini Treat Seats at the table for your dolls, with tiny cups and table settings, too. Look for the box of "Table Talkers," guaranteed to get the conversation rolling (What skill do you have that no one knows about? What is the nicest compliment you've ever gotten? What would you like to be famous for? . . .). And, of course, there are rooms upon rooms of American Girl clothes and accessories, as well as the entire collection of popular books. One warning: most boys will enter here only under duress—be prepared to offer a bribe in the form of a corresponding trip to the nearby **FDNY Fire Zone** (page 45) or **Nintendo World Store** (10 Rockefeller Plaza at 48th Street; 646-459-0800; www.nintendoworldstore.com).

Cool Kid's Corner

Is your American Girl's hair looking a little drab? Bring her down to the Doll Hair Salon where services include brush out and tangle removal, water misting, and ribbon tying. The professional stylists can give your doll a whole new look with a ponytail, half-pony, pigtail, flip, or braided hairstyle. And even if you're not allowed to get your own ears pierced yet, you can get your doll's ears done—and pick a pair of beautiful earrings to complete Kit, Kaya, or Samantha's new look. Sorry, no nail salon yet.

american museum of natural history

❧ *Address: Central Park West at 79th Street*
Phone: 212-769-5100
Ideal Age Group: 5 to 14
Admission: $15 adults / $8.50 children (suggested)
Website: www.amnh.org

Environmentalist Rachel Carson once wrote, "And then there is the world of little things seen all too seldom. Children, perhaps because they themselves are smaller and closer to the ground than we, notice and delight in the small and inconspicuous."

It is precisely this wonderful quality about children that makes visiting the American Museum of Natural History (AMNH) with them such a pleasure. You're pointing out the tall, lethal-looking horns on a herd of gemsbok, while your five-year-old is staring at a hidden snake in the grass. You're fixated on the rippled muscles of the big leopard, while your child wants to know if the little black pig is going to be eaten. It happens every time—just when you think you're going to wow them with the big attraction, kids catch a subtlety that breathes new life into a diorama you've seen fifty times.

Start your visit to AMNH in the Discovery Room, where your kids can jump into scientific discovery by hunting for hidden animals among the branches of a two-story replica of an African baobab tree, assemble more than 200 resin fossil bones into a 14-foot-long replica of a Prestosuchus dinosaur, or track earthquakes in real time anywhere on the planet using seismograph equipment.

After Ben Stiller's family film, *A Night at the Museum*, magically brought this place to life, some kids expect more live action in these hallowed halls. Still, you'll need very little coaxing to get them enthused about the giant Olmec Head with the pudgy face, the moon rocks (definitely not Swiss cheese) in the Ross Hall of Meteorites, or the wild dance costumes in the African Peoples exhibit. One sure to elicit oohs and ahhs is Yahveh, a marvelous costume that's a cross between Chewbacca, the Midas Muffler Man, and a broom. Also, from fall to early spring, children must see the tropical Butterfly Conservatory—a steamy vivarium where literally hundreds of the brightly colored insects flutter around your head and perch on your shoulder to rest. Incredible.

Then it's off to the really BIG exhibits. It's the towering Barosaurus and the dagger-jawed T. rex, along with the rest of the astonishing dinosaurs, that wow children most often. If these fearsome fossils look colossal to you, just imagine how they look from three feet below you. One reminder though: while the immensely popular Fossil Halls will bring you and the kids back again and again, other families have permanently caught Jurassic fever, too. Get here early, just after the bony beasts have had breakfast, and your visit will go along much easier.

Cool Kid's Corner

There's no question that Tyrannosaurus rex and other reptilian earth shakers were ferocious predators. For proof, just take a look at the Allosaurus fossil in the Hall of Saurischian Dinosaurs. You'll see its bones deeply clawed during a savage fight. The horned Triceratops also shows evidence of a massive wound, this one a crushing blow to the left side of its skull. Ouch, I think that Stegosaurus just hit me.

art farm in the city

✳ *Address: 419 East 91st Street between York and 1st Avenues*

Phone: 212-410-3117

Ideal Age Group: 2 to 8

Admission: Day and yearly passes available; classes start at $525 for 15 weeks (depends on semester)

Website: www.theartfarms.org

I have a city friend who went to kindergarten in the country. Whenever she shares stories of feeding local barnyard animals and eating lunch with her classmates under orchard trees, I feel sorry for urban kids who never get a chance to sing the praises of Old MacDonald's Farm.

They have solved this country-mouse, city-mouse dilemma at the one-of-a-kind Art Farm. Here, they masterfully combine what kids love most—animals, art, music, and . . . well, cookies. Baking to be precise.

Created to provide city kids with a country-like atmosphere, just blocks from their apartments, this three-thousand-square-foot refuge is the only indoor farm and petting zoo in Manhattan. Each of the activity rooms is painted to evoke a sense of outdoor life and nature, with a cool mountain lake in the music room, fields of hearty sunflowers in the kitchen and crafts area, and an apple orchard growing cheerfully up the walls of the big basement space.

Co-owner Valentina Van Hise, who holds a degree in music education, has created just the right balance of stimulating recreation and educational activities at the Art Farm. She and her capable young farm hands—who wear overalls and gingham shirts while guiding the under-eight crowd in music, baking, crafts and animal care classes—have a passion and preference for high-quality, adult-child interaction over high-tech distractions. The result is a pace that's decidedly slower (after all, you have to be quiet and patient when stroking a dove's tail feathers), which I believe children find comforting.

While the music classes are highly interactive and fun (choose your music maker from dozens of bins), the art classes original and imaginative (making an animal mask of paper, paint, glitter and feathers is a favorite) and the baking classes a popular pastime (pretzels, cinnamon buns, cookies and muffins are often on the menu), the obvious draw here is the fantastic menagerie. What kid on the planet can resist cuddling a rabbit, petting an incredibly soft chinchilla, watching a parrot fly inches overhead, or touching the rough, cold skin of a bearded dragon lizard? Pass through the red-and-white Dutch doors of the downstairs farm and all this is possible.

Goats, sheep, chickens, ducks and pigs only visit the farm for birthday parties and special occasions, but there are still plenty of feathered and furry friends to keep kids occupied. Want to hold your first tarantula (don't worry, this one is venom-free), let a giant millipede with three hundred legs crawl up your arm, or look into the big eyes of a little gecko? Just ask the animal caretaker who's always on hand, and you can.

When school is out, The Art Farm has an extensive summer camp program for kids ages three to eight where they can spend half or full days baking pizzas, petting snakes, watching magic shows, and learning a lot about animal care.

Cool Kid's Corner

Did you know that pet hamsters like the ones they have at the Art Farm sleep during the day and work out at night on their exercise wheels? Girl hamsters can run up to ten miles in a single night. Boy hamsters don't go as far. They average only one mile . . . then it's back to bed for them!

asphalt green
aquacenter

❊ *Address: 555 East 90th Street at York Avenue*
Phone: 212-369-8890
Ideal Age Group: 2 to 14
Admission: $10 children for drop-in swim (check website
for seasonal classes and annual memberships)
Website: www.asphaltgreen.org

I have fond memories of splashing my way through summer
days at the community swim club. The pool was nothing fancy,
just a few lap lanes, open swim areas, and diving boards that
launched a thousand backflips and cannonballs. We played
Marco Polo and dove for pennies until the tips of our fingers
looked like white raisins. That pool was cool.

Unfortunately, New York City isn't the suburbs, with its
plethora of backyard pools and natural swimming holes. The
city has only a few public pools, which are sometimes unclean,
unsafe and overcrowded, too. What's a little fish to do?

Grab the swimsuits and nose plugs and anchor the family
at the best indoor pool in the city—Asphalt Green's Aqua-
Center. Built in 1993 and renovated in 2007, this contemporary
complex sits next to the cool-looking and architecturally
significant shell of the former Municipal Asphalt Plant—hence
the "Asphalt." "Green" refers to the regulation-sized, artificial
turf soccer field that forms the emerald core of this handsome
sports fitness facility, and is available for free walk-on use.

The large, chlorine-clean aquatics area is a wonderland
for water lovers, refreshingly painted in a get-you-in-the-spirit
aquamarine blue. Asphalt Green has two magnificent pools—
a 50-meter Olympic-size pool that has been host to major
competitions, and a depth-adjustable, 18-by-26-foot sister

pool used for water babies classes and confidence-building kid swims. The therapeutic waters of this smaller exercise pool are kept at a toasty 90° F.

Parents are free to watch the family frogs from a dry spectator gallery overlooking the pools, but it's much more fun to get water logged with the kids, taking your belly flops and playing those dipping and dunking games. The AquaCenter also has kickboards and pool buoys, along with those brightly colored foam noodles for keeping kids afloat. If your child is a serious water sprite, enroll him or her in the innovative swim school classes geared to every level from doggie paddlers to fearless backstrokers. Asphalt Green also offers a free swim instruction program called "Waterproofing," which has taught 27,000 New York City public school kids over the past 15 years how to go from landlubber to recreational fish.

The adjacent, parabola-shaped Murphy Center is a multi-sport training facility with a basketball gym, gymnastics rooms, an elevated indoor running track, and more. The Murphy Center is also home to the **Lenny Suib Puppet Playhouse** (555 East 90th Street at York Avenue; 212-369-8890), where you're guaranteed a world-class weekend puppet performance in an intimate, 100-seat theater.

Cool Kid's Corner

You won't believe this, but the floor of the Olympic-size pool here is hydraulic, meaning it can move up and down automatically. In a matter of minutes, one end can go from six-feet deep to a shallow three feet. It can even be raised to zero feet. Imagine if you could do that in your bathtub—water would splash all over the floor!

books of wonder

❋ *Address: 18 West 18th Street between Fifth and Sixth Avenues*
Phone: 212-989-3270
Ideal Age Group: 2 to 10
Admission: Free story readings Sundays at noon
Website: www.booksofwonder.com

In his fascinating classic, *The Read-Aloud Handbook*, Jim Trelease presents compelling evidence that the practice of reading to children is essential for awakening young imaginations, improving language skills, and even bringing families closer together. He goes further to cite a National Academy of Education study that concluded, "The single most important activity for building the knowledge required for eventual success in reading is reading aloud to children."

The facts are irrefutable—a child who is read to consistently becomes a better reader, and good early readers go on to be enthusiastic students. There's even evidence that prenatal reading has a positive effect on a child's learning potential. All of which is overshadowed by the simple fact that reading aloud is fun for both adult and child.

My observation is that parents are reading to children like never before. But when you're simply maxed out on picture books, or run low on reading steam, there's help available from a few excellent bookstores offering regular children's storybook hours—sometimes embellished with appearances by lovable storybook characters in costume.

Books of Wonder, the last dedicated children's bookstore in the city, has been a reliable friend to kids who love stories since 1980, offering delightful Sunday presentations in a clean, pleasant environment. The store's friendly, animated readers have access to thousands of titles in this bright, colorful store, so your children are always exposed to the best in classic and contemporary picture books. And for an after-story treat, amble over to the **Cupcake Café** inside the store (212-465-1530, www.cupcakecafe-nyc.com) where they not only serve pretty baked treats with real butter crème frosting, they have these cool ladybug seats and circular benches so your kids can sprawl out happily with a good book and a bite.

Parents will also note that Books of Wonder has one the largest selections of collectible and rare children's books in the city, including all those we loved: The Hardy Boys, Nancy Drew, The Bobsy Twins, along with early editions of Frank Baum's *The Wonderful Wizard of Oz*.

If Books of Wonder's downtown location is inconvenient, you might prefer the Saturday or Sunday morning readings at **Barnes & Noble** (240 East 86th Street at 2nd Avenue; 212-794-1962; www.barnesandnoble.com). Check with your local library, too. They often have a children's reading nook with a scheduled story hour each week.

Cool Kid's Corner

Some of your favorite children's authors and illustrators come to Books of Wonder just to see you. Check the website for a calendar of appearances by best-selling writers like J.K. Rowling (*Harry Potter* series), Chris Van Allsburg (*The Polar Express, Jumanji*), Eric Carle (*The Very Hungry Caterpillar*), Mo Willems (*Don't Let The Pigeon Drive The Bus*), plus illustrators Bryan Collier (*Doo-Wop Pop*) and Hillary Knight (the *Eloise* stories).

bronx zoo

❊ *Address: Bronx River Parkway at Fordham Road, Bronx*
Phone: 718-367-1010
Ideal Age Group: 2 to 14
Admission: Call or check Website for combination venue pricing
Website: www.bronxzoo.com

Just when you think nothing could be cuter than your own puppy or kitten, a baby gorilla is born at the Bronx Zoo and the whole world comes down with "adorable ape disease." In fact, this remarkable zoo's natural habitats often become wildlife nurseries, with sea lion pups, infant fruit bats, little lizards, baby squirrel monkeys, and lovable tiger cubs stealing your heart.

If those little fellows don't win you over, the largest urban zoo in the country will get you with about four thousand other animals, all kept within the zoo's spectacularly designed 265 acres. In the African Plains exhibit alone, you'll get a close-up look at magnificent lions roaming the savanna, along with graceful gazelles, leggy storks, stripy zebras, and those gangly giraffes—I've always wondered how the world would look from 18 feet up.

The famous World of Reptiles has the kind of slithery attractions that children never forget—like gigantic pythons and venomous snakes. If you're raising a young zoologist with a fondness for monkeys, walk over to JungleWorld, an Asian rain forest setting that's home to playful gibbons, as well as a pair of intense black panthers. And pray that your noggin doesn't look like a ripe mango, because broad-winged fruit bats dart freely just inches above your head.

The Bengali Express, a guided monorail tour that passes over Wild Asia, offers a close-up look at young rhinos and rare silka deer. The queue for this train adventure can be long, but once on the open-sided cars, close encounters with powerful elephants and regal Indo-Chinese tigers make the wait worthwhile. Other "don't miss" attractions include the Madagascar exhibit with the 800-pound Nile Crocodiles (don't let their massive grins and lazy dispositions fool you—they can outrun a person over short distances) and the spectacular, three-season Butterfly Garden.

If you're escorting children under seven, zip over to the Children's Zoo (separate fee for adults and kids), with its mulch-lined walkways that are gentler on a child's easily fatigued legs. The general theme at this mini-zoo is "do as the animals do." So when I go, I make myself very small to squeeze through the prairie dog tunnels in a dirt mound adjacent to the real thing (fun, but best left to tinier bodies). Then I take the leap test to see if I can jump farther than a bullfrog (the frog always wins), or I crawl inside one of three human-sized turtle shells. Finally, I like to stop by the petting zoo, buy a handful of food pellets that look like Grape Nuts and let a brown llama tickle my palm with its soft muzzle.

Cool Kid's Corner

Ever wonder what it would feel like to be a lizard escaping down a hollow tree? You can find out at the Children's Zoo, where they've placed a slippery spiral slide inside a giant imitation oak. Just climb the stairs to the tree house and take the long ride down. After four topsy-turvy descents during a recent visit, my friend had to drag me away.

brooklyn children's museum

❊ *Address: 145 Brooklyn Avenue at St. Marks Avenue, Brooklyn*
Phone: 718-735-4400
Ideal Age Group: 2 to 10
Admission: $7.50 per person
Website: www.brooklynkids.org

After a major renovation that doubled its size, the Brooklyn Children's Museum reopened in the fall of 2008. Now, the new yolk-yellow building is a homing beacon for every kid within the five boroughs.

Founded in 1899, the Brooklyn Children's Museum was the world's first museum created just for kids. With 110 years of experience, the folks here really know how to make an impression on young minds. What's the coolest part of this re-imagined museum? How about the fact that it's NYC's first "green" museum? With everyone thinking about their carbon footprint, this museum now has one as small as its visitors' shoe sizes.

The most exciting of the exhibits for the museum's youngest guests is the all-new Totally Tots area, which has enough cool stuff to incite jealousy among elder siblings (you only get to play in this space if you're five years old or younger). Designed by a kid-minded duo of installation artists, Totally Tots has a monster box of bright, sparkling blue sand at one end (the color of Cookie Monster), and a feat of engineering called Water Wonders at the other—complete with water pumps, pools, showers sprays, boats and a place for splashing without getting totally soaked. Distributed between these popular stations are places where kids can put on puppet shows, create art in the brightly colored studio, sprawl on pillows in a cozy reading tent, or do what seemed to attract the largest kid crowd at Totally Tots—bang on pots, pans, and other ad hoc instruments in a riotous orchestra.

If you've visited the Brooklyn Children's Museum in years past, then you surely remember the corrugated metal tunnel, illuminated by neon lights with a 100-foot long sluiceway (that manmade babbling creek) running down its length. It's still there, and it's still a popular runway for kids charging up and down the museum's action-packed floors, looking for a place to expend more energy. Follow the kids down the tube, and go check out Neighborhood Nature to see what kinds of trees grow in Brooklyn, what plants grow in urban community gardens, and much more. We're so concrete-oriented in NYC that sometimes we forget that Brooklyn has beachfront property, too. It's really neat to see and hear the sounds of the ocean in this exhibit, along with the local critters that live in places like Prospect Park.

Tired of being inside? Head out to the greenhouse when the season permits and visit the kid-tended gardens for a breath of fresh air. You'll be greeted by an aromatic burst of fresh basil, which might make you crave a slice of pizza. No problem, just head back inside to the new World Brooklyn exhibit, where you can see how that perfect melange of cheese, sauce, dough and basil are fashioned into the borough's famous pizza pies.

Cool Kid's Corner

Don't forget to look for the bus! Almost life-sized, this city bus has a huge steering wheel that you can grab and spin. There are all the usual bells and whistles of a city bus, but it's much more exciting because every rider on your bus is a kid, and no one is being driven around on boring errands. Nope, on this bus you can decide to go wherever your imagination takes you.

central park threebies

❈ *Address: See specific locations below*

Phone: 212-860-1370

Ideal Age Group: 3 to 12

Admission: Free, or almost free

Website: www.centralparknyc.org

The Carousel, Belvedere Castle, and the Dana Discovery Center are three gems within Central Park that are also free (or almost so). Many an afternoon can be spent enjoying this satisfying trio.

Everyone loves the **Central Park Carousel** (Mid-Central Park at 64th Street; 212-879-0244; www.centralparkcarousel.com)— a classic, turn-of-the-century merry-go-round. Built in 1903 by the eminent wood-carvers, Stein and Goldstein, it features 58 hand-carved horses, colorful chariots, and plump cherubs. The four-minute ride only costs $2, and includes the traditional piped-in organ music, which will take you back to the golden age of carnivals. In New York, we say no childhood is complete without ten to twenty annual visits to this famous carousel. Merry-go-round nirvana can also be reached in Brooklyn at the **Prospect Park Carousel** (Prospect Park at Ocean Avenue; 718-282-7789; www.prospectpark.org).

When children get within a hundred paces of **Belvedere Castle** (Mid-Central Park at 79th Street; www.centralparknyc .com), they break into a run, eager to explore this regal, medieval-like structure in Central Park. Originally designed as a Victorian "folly," or a place for playfulness and fantasy, it doesn't disappoint. Situated on Vista Rock, the second highest elevation in the park, visitors have feasted their eyes on the surrounding pastoral beauty from here since 1872 (the castle was restored to its original nineteenth-century splendor in the early 1980s).

For children, Belvedere Castle is a storybook come to life. There's a moat (the Turtle Pond), ramparts (the stone outcropping it sits on), parapets, turrets, a dragon crest over the door, and a narrow circular staircase leading to the main tower. Open year-round, Belvedere Castle works as the perfect backdrop for fantasy play. Step back and let your kids get on with their Renaissance faire.

After the castle, head north to the **Dana Discovery Center** (Central Park at 110th Street; www.centralparknyc.org), where you and the kids can sit on the shaded bank of a quiet lake, fishing poles dangling over the water, large-mouth bass flirting with your bait.

The lake here was transformed by landscape architect Laura Starr, who teamed up with the Central Park Conservancy to transform the eleven-acre Harlem Meer from a debris-filled swamp into a stunning nature area with wetlands and a sandy beach. The visitor center is filled with free activities for kids year-round—including environmental education, arts-and-crafts workshops, holiday programs (don't miss the Halloween Pumpkin Sail), hands-on science projects and fishing! The lake is stocked with more than 50,000 bass, catfish, shiners, and bluegills for kids to catch and release from mid-April through mid-October. Poles, bait, and all the enrichment programs here are free.

Cool Kid's Corner

For a good chuckle, watch the adoring faces of parents and grandparents at the Carousel each time their child makes a merry revolution. Eyes go buggy, mouths open hilariously, and heads tilt back slightly with each abrupt intake of breath. It's the "carousel face!"

central park zoo

※ *Address: Central Park at 64th Street*
Phone: 212-439-6500
Ideal Age Group: 2 to 12
Admission: $8 adults / $3 children
Website: www.centralparkzoo.com

This past summer, I visited Tanzania in Africa and had the awesome experience of going on safari. Every day I was within a few yards of elephants, giraffes, hippos, zebras, even lions. It made me appreciate how special it is to see wild animals in natural habitats where they are protected, safe, and free.

Which brings me to the venerable Central Park Zoo. Some people are uncomfortable with animals being displayed in small urban zoos, and I share some of those concerns. But this little gem in the center of Manhattan is part of the Wildlife Conservation Society. The WCS is obsessively focused on the welfare of their wild residents, and the animals living here are carefully selected based upon their space requirements and how the zoo can accommodate those needs. What results is a magical place where animals are meticulously cared for and children always have a captivating experience.

Even if you live in the city and have visited the zoo a hundred times, make it a hundred and one—there's always more for you and your kids to discover here. I never saw the tree-napping red pandas until my fourth trip, and I often find peculiar new critters in the Rain Forest who were hiding on previous visits. I love to watch young "veterans" of the zoo confidently escorting their smaller siblings along the richly landscaped paths to see the "ice bears" or the monkeys with the "red tushies." This zoo is particularly well suited to tiny bodies with little feet, because they can meander easily through the entire compact habitat in a short time.

First, stop in the Rain Forest where you'll find hundreds of monkeys (the white-maned tamarins will charm you), reptiles, and tropical birds, along with tanks of exotic fish. This steamy, two-story natural jungle—an ideal antidote for cold winter days—also houses a humongous ant farm where children can watch thousands of leaf-cutter ants dart through deep catacombs, via miniature closed-circuit camera.

From here, children usually dash to favorite destinations like the polar bear exhibit where Gus and Ida, the internationally known swimming duo, enjoy their frigid laps while kids stare from behind glass walls just a paw's distance away. I also like the shivery "Edge of the Ice Pack" because I can't get enough of those zippy penguins shooting out of the water bolt upright onto the rocky shoreline.

Your entrance ticket to the Central Park Zoo includes admission to the ever-popular **Tisch Children's Zoo**, just a two-minute walk across the pedestrian path. Designed for children 6 and under, your littlest animal lovers will be thrilled to pet and feed gentle goats, pot-bellied pigs, sheep, cows, and other farm animals through split rail fences.

Cool Kid's Corner

Before you leave the neighborhood, stop by the zoo's north gate below the Delacorte Clock. Every half hour as the time is chimed, you can watch the slow pirouettes of an elephant on accordion, a hippo playing the violin, a mountain goat tooting a flute, a penguin beating a drum, a dancing bear with a tambourine, and a horn-blowing Mama kangaroo with her baby. And, of course, the playful pair of monkeys on top, thumping the bell!

chelsea piers sports & entertainment complex

❊ *Address: On the piers from 17th to 23rd Street along the Hudson River*

Phone: 212-336-6666

Ideal Age Group: 2 to 14

Admission: Free to piers / Activities as low as $10 for general skating access

Website: www.chelseapiers.com

This gigantic waterfront sports and recreation center was built on the kind of scale New Yorkers love—"the only" scale. Chelsea Piers has the only four-story, year-round golf driving range in the country, the only indoor ice skating rinks in Manhattan (one each for hockey and figure skating), and the only gymnastics training area in New York City sanctioned for competition by USA Gymnastics. In the "tallest" and "longest" categories, Chelsea Piers has one of the tallest rock climbing walls in the Northeast and one of the world's longest indoor running tracks, at a quarter mile.

If you're familiar with the imposing size of skyscrapers, you can best comprehend the sheer mass of this complex by thinking of four eighty-story buildings lying down. Stretched over historic shipping piers, all 1.7 million square feet are designed to deliver peak, high-energy fun for sports-starved children and adults, whether you're into bowling or baseball, driving golf balls or taking dance classes.

The central attraction for kids is the main Field House, with two indoor soccer fields, a 28-foot rock climbing wall specially designed for children, basketball courts, four batting cages ($2 for ten swings), plus a massive gymnastics facility (in-ground trampoline, rings, pommel horses, balance beams, parallel bars, you name it). Be sure to take a plunge into the foam-filled diving pit, too, but hang onto your pocket change.

The impressive Sky Rink was the catalyst for Chelsea Piers. Developer Roland Betts was looking for a practice facility for his figure-skating daughter, Jessie. Good father that he was, Betts got some friends together, borrowed $120 million, and erected this mega sports mall. Now his daughter plus every other kid in New York can turn figure eights 22 hours a day.

I've never been to an Olympic Sports Village, but it must be a lot like this—safe, sanitized, steeped in primary colors, with athletes of every age, from around the world, walking around in Under Armor workout wear, looking fit and healthy. The user-friendly Chelsea Piers is such a total sports resource, that a number of area schools have abandoned their on-premises physical education programs and bussed their kids over here for an absolute field day.

Cool Kid's Corner

I don't see many little kids walking around the city with their golf bags (on the other hand, Tiger Woods must have started young), but whether you own clubs or not, drag your duffer dad or mom over to the four floors of ball whacking wildness at the Chelsea Piers Golf Club. You won't believe your eyes when those little white balls are teed up for you automatically. They're machine-retrieved from the 250-yard driving range, too.

children's museum of the arts

❊ *Address: 182 Lafayette Street between Broome and Grand Streets*
Phone: 212-274-0986
Ideal Age Group: 2 to 12
Admission: $9 per person / $200 per family, per year for unlimited visits
Website: www.cmany.org

When I saw the life-sized zebra on the sidewalk I knew I had found the Children's Museum of the Arts (CMA), but I didn't really arrive until a giddy three-year-old handed me a heaping cup of yellow flubber. So much for my note taking—within minutes I was sitting next to my pint-sized friend at a low-lying art table creating a lumpy sculpture out of the slippery stuff.

That's what they do best at this informal, vibrant space in SoHo—they bring out the spontaneous creative spirit that thrives inside every child. CMA is the city's only hands-on art museum for children, which means your kids can express themselves through dozens of messy mediums during daily art projects, including paint, pastels, collage, sand painting, clay sculpture, origami, and more. While exploring their creative potential, your little Picassos will be mentored by at least three adult facilitators, all trained artists themselves.

The special environment here is guaranteed to stimulate your child's senses with two floors of art and crafts tables, mini-performance areas, reading nooks, and interactive exhibitions that submerge kids in exuberant creation. If there is any question that this formula succeeds, just check out the stroller parking lot by the entrance, or the four-foot-high wooden shoe filled with countless pairs of Stride Rites and kid Crocs.

Little kids don't know much about formal art, but they know if you stick half a dozen jars of tempera paints in front of them with permission to smear the colorful contents all over a tabletop, it's going to be a blast. Here, children are encouraged to be expressive, independent, playful, and passionate as they experiment with artwork—which basically means anything goes. In fact, the informal motto at CMA is: You Can Smell It, Touch It, And Play With It, Just Don't Eat It.

On the lower level, children often swarm to a fantastic play corral called the ball pond. Surrounded by a brilliant blue mural of underwater images, girls and boys get bouncy, throwing their bodies with obvious pleasure into dozens of huge blue, green, and orange rubber balls. This is ideal for working large muscles and helping kids blow off steam before sitting down to a focused art project. And if your toddler loves to make art, listen to stories, and make loud music with clanging pans, kooky kazoos, and chichi maracas, ask about the multi-sensory Wee-Arts Program.

I also wanted to tell you about the giant blackboard table for non-stop chalk art, the self-portrait area, and the twelve-foot dragon made of coffee cans, but now I'm pooped. So just go to CMA and make art!

Cool Kid's Corner

Flubber is fun and you can make it at home with this simple recipe: Put ten drops of food coloring into a cup of hot water. Add one cup of school glue. Dissolve two tablespoons of 20 Mule Team Borax into a separate $1/3$ cup of water. Pour the Borax solution into the glue/water mixture and STIR IMMEDIATELY. Let sit for two to four hours and that's it—you've just made safe, nontoxic flubber!

conservatory garden

※ *Address: 105th Street and Fifth Avenue*
　Phone: 212-860-1382
　Ideal Age Group: 3 to 12
　Admission: Free
　Website: www.centralparknyc.org

Any kid with a good imagination (that would be every child you know) approaches the mighty wrought iron fence that encircles the Conservatory Garden with eye-popping anticipation. Never mind that there is not a seesaw or slide in sight at this spectacular, six-acre formal garden. The precisely planted flower beds, arbor-covered walkways, perfectly manicured lawns, and two sculpted fountains supply plenty of fantasy fodder . . . think *The Secret Garden* and you'll understand.

Set off from the rest of Central Park by the impressive Vanderbilt Gate (taken from the family's former mansion on 58th Street) and sitting below street level, the Conservatory Garden has a stately presence, a magical not-in-New-York quality that appeals to children. Little countesses and counts love to imagine that they're skipping through the grounds of an English palace. A race up the steps to the western pergola is fun, too, as is watching the pair of fountains spurt and splash with dancing water patterns. On spring and summer weekends, wedding parties use the garden as a bucolic backdrop for photographs, which has made the Conservatory Garden a popular destination for bride watching. And you don't have to be a girl with a Wedding Bell Barbie to appreciate the ritual pomp of these spectacles.

The Conservatory Garden, which takes its name from a huge glass conservatory that covered this same spot from 1898 until 1934, is actually three gardens in one, representing Italian,

French, and English landscape styles. But in every section of the garden you'll find a quality of carefree safety, as well as secluded niches, hedge-hidden benches and snaking paths that call out for exploration. A particularly fun game is seeking out the sidewalk medallions inscribed with the names of the original 13 colonies.

Another unusual offering of the Conservatory Garden is a place to sit quietly with your child, flanked by crab apple trees swaying to gentle breezes. Andy Rooney, the cranky *60 Minutes* commentator, once wrote that walks around the block with his father on summer nights during his childhood did wonders for him as an adult. Carry a good storybook into this pristine setting on a spring day (when thousands of multicolored tulips are in bloom), set yourself down with your favorite four-year-old on a sweet and shady bench, and you'll make an equally lasting impression on your young charge.

The Urban Park Rangers (800-201-PARK) offer an active schedule of outdoor workshops, guided walks, and activities for kids conducted throughout our city parks department. Also note the close proximity of the **Dana Discovery Center** (page 34) just five blocks north, where they have exceptional nature programs for children all year.

Cool Kid's Corner

If you've read Frances Hodgson Burnett's *The Secret Garden*, go quickly to the south end fountain where a bronze Mary and Dickon are playing mischievously. I heard some children say they saw elves and fairies stepping on the fountain's lily pads. Look, there they are!

empire state building observatory

❋ *Address: 350 Fifth Avenue between 33rd and 34th Streets*

Phone: 212-736-3100/877-NYC-VIEW

Ideal Age Group: 5 to 14

Admission: $19 adults / $13 children for observatory; $40 adults / $19 children for observatory and NY Skyride combo ticket

Website: www.esbnyc.com

During a class trip in the fifth grade, some friends and I were peering over the edge of the outdoor observation deck on the 86th floor of the Empire State Building (ESB). A uniformed guard approached and told us to step back. Then, as if to stress the awesome destructive power of a building this tall, he said something that has stuck in my brain for years: "You know, if you dropped a penny from up here it would imbed itself five inches deep in the sidewalk."

True or not, his words added to the formidable mystique of the world's most famous building, and prompted me to buy one of those five-inch scale souvenirs of the quarter-mile-high skyscraper. That memento sat on my desk next to a bronze replica of the Liberty Bell (Philadelphia class trip, sixth grade) until I left for college.

Sure, lots of cities can claim sky-high buildings, but there's only one original skyscraper—only one famous pencil point where King Kong swatted down rickety biplanes and Tom Hanks returned for Jonah's backpack and got the girl in *Sleepless in Seattle* (yes, I've seen *An Affair to Remember*, but what kid remembers?). The Empire State Building's multiple observation decks and central location also give children the most visual bang for their buck, as they pick out notable sights at every compass point and identify the five states visible from here—let me see, New Jersey, Pennsylvania, Connecticut, Massachusetts and, duhhh . . . New York!

There are 73 elevators in this building, but for some reason not one of them goes directly to the 86th floor, making a trip to the observatory an adventure in itself. You have to go to the 80th floor, trek through office hallways, then finish the trip in a second elevator—all of which seems to punctuate the building's enormous size (ESB actually has its own zip code!). Of course, there are those great night lights, too. Every evening, the tower is bathed in a unique color palette—a changing lighting scheme synchronized to special events, holidays and happenings (the daily Tower Lights schedule is posted on the website).

Keep in mind that this is one of the world's most popular tourist attractions with long lines that can really bum kids out. Try an early arrival at 8 A.M. or visit at dinner hour, between 5 P.M. and 8 P.M. Or as an excellent alternative, consider visiting the open-air, **Top of the Rock Observation Deck** (30 Rockefeller Plaza at 50th Street; 212-698-2000; www.topoftherocknyc.com). You'll still get those awesome, 360-degree views of the city and beyond, but at the Rock they offer timed tickets in advance— which mean no lines, no waiting, and no cranky kids.

Cool Kid's Corner

At ESB, ask your parents nicely to purchase a combination ticket for the **NY Skyride** (Second Floor; 888-759-7433; www.skyride.com). Then sit down, strap in, and hang on for a fast-flying virtual tour, a big screen thrill ride that takes you over and under 30 great city sights. Synchronized to the on-screen action, your seat sways, rolls, dips and dives for an excellent, in-your-face New York adventure.

FDNY fire zone

*Address: 34 West 51st Street between Fifth and
Sixth Avenues*
Phone: 212-698-4520
Ideal Age Group: 5 to 9
Admission: General Admission is Free; Fire-Safety
Presentation is $6 per person
Website: www.fdnyfirezone.org

Do your children know exactly what to do, where to go, and whom to call if they smell smoke in your home? Billy Blazes, leader of the Rescue Heroes, and Hot Dog, the fire safety dog, are two friends down at the FDNY Fire Zone who can teach them.

Fire safety education is so important for kids, and it's delivered in such a unique, fun, and multi-sensory way at the Fire Zone, that I suggest you bring the whole family here at least once. House fires are the leading cause of fire fatalities in this country, and studies show that a little education can go a long way in preventing them. At the Fire Zone, they use all the same tricks that media masters employ to ensure that your children leave with memorable, life-saving messages—quick tips that they'll never forget in an emergency.

Created by the same innovative set designers who worked on the former hit Broadway show *Cats*, the facility's faux firehouse design and high-tech, multimedia experience are intended to grab and hold the attention of restless children. It works. The lobby area includes a life-sized, fire truck cutaway where kids can play junior firefighter while pushing buttons, putting on authentic fire gear, listening to emergency dispatches, and testing their fire safety knowledge on interactive video consoles. Every hour on the half-hour, a retired or off-duty firefighter gives an excellent presentation, complete with a race to the fire scene, billowing smoke, real-life video testimonials, and all the facts on creating an escape plan that could get your family out of danger fast.

At the end of the experience, children are guided away from a fake fire to safety through a short, darkened passageway filled with smoke. While it's very brief, harmless and fun (some kids scream in feigned terror), I did observe a child or two under six who became momentarily frightened. Act accordingly.

You spill out into the Fire Zone's well-stocked store, where you can choose from all sorts of official licensed FDNY products with proceeds benefiting the FDNY Foundation. Look on the walls where they've mounted more than twenty-two hundred firehouse patches from around the world. Amazingly, the patch designs and original artwork are almost always created by a talented station firefighter. I guess you could call these people "distinguished extinguishers."

For kids who just have to get their daily dose of Super Mario Brothers or Wii Sports, there's good news. The Fire Zone is just blocks from the **Nintendo World Store** (10 Rockefeller Plaza at 48th Street; 646-459-0800), also the official headquarters of everything Pokémon.

Cool Kid's Corner

If you remember nothing else, remember this: If your hair or clothes catch on fire, "Stop, Drop and Roll!" If you see smoke, call 911 immediately, then "Get Low and Go!" And even if you're scared, "Don't Hide, Get Outside!" Ask for Hot Dog's free FDNY coloring book and Billy Blazes' Fire Escape Game for these tips and more.

hippo playground

❊ *Address: Riverside Drive at 91st Street*

Phone: 212-870-3070

Ideal Age Group: 2 to 7

Admission: Free

Website: www.riversideparkfund.org

Near the library of the small North Jersey town where I grew up, we had a thumb-sized park with a big green concrete frog poised to leap out the front gate. He was such a sweet frog, so agreeable when hundreds of drooling toddlers climbed on his head and slid down his back, that the playground was fondly and forever christened Froggie Park.

I imagine it is with this same nostalgic fondness that every child who has ever played at Hippo Playground remembers this friendly neighborhood playground when they grow too big for happy hippos. Why hippos? Nobody knows. Maybe because it's a funny name kids love to say. In any case, they arrived in 1993 and they're here to stay—seven adult hippos and six baby hippos, all frozen in various stages of wading and wallowing, some bellowing, others belching a spray fountain of water.

Even watching the park's smallest visitors, it's clear that hippos are happening. I saw an 18-month-old face off with a big bull, shout some unintelligible demands at him with broad gestures, slap him on his wide snout, then march away. Like my Froggie, he was tolerant to the end.

One unusual aspect of this very safe park is that it's cooperatively maintained by the Parks Department and an all-volunteer community group called the Hippo Playground Project. Consisting primarily of local parents, this hardworking group raises funds for upkeep and improvements in the park and sponsors creative programming like "Art in the Park" for kids during the summer, as well as a series of autumn activities.

Besides the hippopotami, this oval-shaped, intimate playground is ideally designed for kids under seven, with ADA accessible swings, plenty of conventional swings with safety surfaces underneath, a sandbox (the clean, asbestos-free sand is replaced regularly), a spray fountain, creative adventure play equipment, four slides including a neat spiral model, and a comfort station—all shaded by magnificent 50-year-old oaks. Because the playground is fenced and attended, it's possible for parents to read a book or take some sun without having to constantly monitor children. After a winter snow, the big hill on the east side of the playground is also a popular kids' sledding area (I wonder if it's called Hippopotamus Hill?).

Here is every child's favorite thing to do at Hippo Playground: Go to the center cluster of adult hippos and scream as loud as you want into the big bull's cavernous mouth. Smaller kids can finish off by climbing down his throat and sliding out his belly.

Cool Kid's Corner

For special fun, run to the big boulder at the south end of the playground. Now look closely and see if you can find the little animals clinging to the rock—three bronze turtles, three frogs, two snakes, the rat eating a snake, a bird, and a tiny mouse. They may be hiding, but they're all there—I promise.

intrepid sea-air-space museum

✳ *Address: Pier 86 at West 46th Street on the Hudson River*
212-245-0072
Ideal Age Group: 6 to 14
Admission: $19.50 adults / $14.50 children, under 5 free
Website: www.intrepidmuseum.org

After a two year, $80 million spit shine, the legendary *Intrepid* aircraft carrier was "reberthed" on Manhattan's west side in the fall of 2008 and looks ready for redeployment. The silent power of this decommissioned, World War II-era flattop, loaded with hundreds of fighter planes and military artifacts from our nation's wartime history, once again renders children awestruck.

The *Intrepid* has a heroic record of Navy service during World War II and Vietnam. In addition to being an astronaut recovery vessel for the early NASA missions. Now, part of the world's largest naval museum, the *Intrepid*'s cavernous interior hangars (three football fields long) are filled with the latest interactive exhibits and multi-sensory thrills. You can experience a smoke-and-flame-filled attack by kamikazes (the *Intrepid* was hit four times in WWII), explore areas of the ship never before open to the public, like the Anchor and Chain room and officers' sleeping quarters, walk in the shadow of stubby-nosed Grumman war planes, and shoehorn your body into the cockpit of an actual A-6 Intruder fighter jet.

The new Exploreum really rocks. Try the Cargo Climb where you scamper up hull-hanging cargo nets just like sailors do. Use the ship's brass Talk Tubes to communicate with other "shipmates." Lie upside down in the cockpit of a Gemini space capsule and work the controls. Or see if you can stay afloat in a mini-lifeboat that sways and pitches like it's bobbing on the high seas. Young history buffs can meet actual *Intrepid* veterans on the ship's command bridge, where former WWII sailors share wonderful tales of the aircraft carrier's adventures as a gaggle of polished bronze instruments surround them.

Off ship, along the spectacularly rebuilt Pier 86, you've got your choice of a submarine or the supersonic, needle-nosed *Concorde*. My choice for kids would be the USS *Growler*. In this former guided missile sub—the world's only nuclear-deterrent submarine open to the public—children can see the tight quarters where submerged sailors lived for weeks at a time. High points of this claustrophobia tour include the tiny stainless steel showers, sleeping bunks squeezed alongside torpedo bays, and hatch doorways you'll definitely conk your head on unless you're under ten and nimble.

This entire moored monument to America's military might changes often, with new exhibits, frequent visits from active Navy vessels, as well as Fleet Week in May when ships invade from around the world. But there's one deadly sky streaker that's always onboard the *Intrepid*'s upper flight deck (with 30 other restored aircraft), and shouldn't be missed—the Lockheed A-12 *Blackbird*, the highest-flying, fastest aircraft on the planet. This coal black monster flies at Mach 3—triple the speed of sound!

Cool Kid's Corner

For an extra fee, the *Intrepid* has a thrilling Virtual Flight Zone—two motion-based rides that simulate the spinning, spiraling, upside-down cockpit action of dog-fighting jets. Or find one of the many free training consoles throughout the ship, where you can practice flattop landings via video. Turns out, I'm a lousy fighter pilot—I crashed my $65 million jet about ten times. It's off to the brig for me!

kerbs conservatory water sailboats

❊ *Address: Central Park at 74th Street near Fifth Avenue*

Phone: 917-796-1382

Ideal Age Group: 5 to 12

Admission: Sailboat rental $10 per half-hour

E-mail for reservations: sailboatguy@hotmail.com

Website: www.centralpark.com

The Kerbs Conservatory has a timeless quality that is leisurely and agreeable. Sailing a model boat with a young mariner is the kind of activity perfectly paced for an early spring morning or late summer afternoon sojourn. At the Kerbs Conservatory, they even supply the radio-controlled model yachts.

The oval-shaped boat pond sits in a small valley originally intended to be a formal garden with a glass conservatory. But park designers Frederick Law Olmstead and Calvert Vaux ran out of money, so the two-acre basin became a venue for ice-skating and model boat races. In 1929, the pond was rimmed with the low concrete wall you see today, so children can safely lean over and push their boats into the shallow waters.

If you have your own model sailboat, you can use the Conservatory Water for sailing from April through October. You can even store it in the Kerbs Boathouse after securing a $20 season permit (212-360-8133). To rent a boat—available from mid-April through early November—look for Ron McKechnie (the Sailboat Guy), who's been operating his nautical pushcart concession by water's edge for more than 20 years.

Generally, two boats are recommended, one for parent and one for child, so you can stage your own informal races. These model boats have no motors, and the radio controls only move the rudders and sails. Still, with the simple handheld control box, even young children can master the operation of these mini-yachts in minutes. The rental boats, with masts as high as four feet, can also be effective for teaching the basic concepts of sailing to those who've never ventured out on a full-sized Sunfish. Somehow, it's a lot easier to practice tacking maneuvers when you're not worried about getting clocked by the mainsail or tossed overboard.

There are two other attractions close by. The **Hans Christian Andersen Storybook Statue** on the west side of the Conservatory Water has been home to a wonderful summer tradition for more than 50 years—Saturday morning storytelling at 11 A.M. (end of June through September, 212-613-3117). Children will hear engaging myths, fairy tales and legends from around the world. Most days, year-round, you also will find several telescopes set up along the western edge of the pond used by locals and park visitors to observe the activities of **Pale Male** (www.palemale.com) and his honey, Lola—two handsome, red-tailed hawks that reside on the ledges of a swanky Fifth Avenue residence and hunt rodents, pigeons and squirrels in the park.

Cool Kid's Corner

If you want to see some really spectacular model boats with polished wooden hulls and sails as tall as you are, take a peak inside Kerbs Memorial Boathouse (at the Fifth Avenue side of the pond, next to the food stand). That's where the privately owned yachts are stored, many ranging in price from $500 to $5,000. Serious sportsmen race these prized boats on Saturday mornings from 10 A.M.-2 P.M. during the summer months. During those hours, there is no other boating at the Kerbs Conservatory—but there's plenty of expert sailing action to watch.

kerlin learning center at wave hill

✳ *Address: West 249th Street and Independence Avenue, Riverdale, Bronx*

Phone: 718-549-3200

Ideal Age Group: 2 to 10

Admission: $6 adults, $2 children, free for children under 6

Website: www.wavehill.org

Since weekdays are filled with a deluge of play dates, errands, after-school lessons and organized activities, a little respite and relaxation is a welcome change on weekends—even if you're an indefatigable six-year-old.

The Kerlin Learning Center at Wave Hill is perfect for mellowing out with city kids—and every Saturday and Sunday, 52 weekends a year, the Family Art Project here offers the chance to smell, feel, touch, and even taste an unspoiled bit of nature. As they explore the beautiful gardens, spacious lawns, and peaceful wooded trails of this spectacular 28-acre oasis, children learn about the outdoors by being in it—a positive, full-immersion experience that brownstone babies just can't get at the local dog run.

On weekend afternoons from 1 to 4 P.M., your children are placed in the capable hands of visual artist and naturalist, Noah Baen. Since 1990, Noah has guided kids through Wave Hill's lush landscape, pointing out the shapes of leaves, the fragrances of flowers, the buzzing and fluttering of bees, butterflies, and birds. In the winter, when nature seems to sleep, Noah cleverly rolls back a big rock to see what crawls out, or finds life on the end of a tree branch where none seemed to exist a moment before.

Then the kids collect stuff: pinecones, seed pods, dry grasses, flower petals, chipped rocks, red berries, twisted gourds, variegated leaves, and all sorts of other wondrous outdoor bounty. Under Noah's watchful eye, this collection is creatively transformed by the children into art: floral collages, ornamental wreaths, handmade paper, natural noisemakers, three-dimensional paintings, traditional corn husk dolls, and harvest headdresses. Much of this inspiring work can be found festooning the walls and hanging from the ceiling of the Kerlin Learning Center, located in Wave Hill's main facility—an impressive stone mansion built in 1843.

Noah is a superb teacher and respectful friend to the children who drop in for his inspiring, sensory workshops. He thinks nothing of wearing a butterfly wing hat to enhance a story about monarch migration, or a leaf mask to explain the miracle of fall foliage. Best of all, he offers each child his focused attention and enthusiastically admires every creation. That's a special gift.

Cool Kid's Corner

Noah creates unforgettable seasonal festivals like the one in September called Buzz-O-Rama. It takes place near the active outdoor honeybee hives at Wave Hill where you might make a cool bee costume, pick up a pollination wand at the Pollination Information Station, and become a bumblebee living in a giant cardboard hive. There's even a guest beekeeper who will give you a taste of the yummy honey right off the waxy comb.

liberty helicopters

✣ *Address: Westside Heliport at 30th Street and 12th Avenue (also Downtown Manhattan Heliport at Pier 6 and the East River)*

Phone: 212-967-6464; 800-542-9933

Ideal Age Group: 4 to 14

Admission: Varying tours from $110 to $204 per person (children under 35 lbs. fly free sitting on an adult lap)

Website: www.libertyhelicopters.com

Long ago, when the MetLife tower in midtown Manhattan (formerly the Pan Am Building) had a heliport on its roof, my mother took my sister and me on a whirlybird tour of the city. It made such an impression that I can close my eyes today and still feel the lurching liftoff of my first helicopter ride.

Today, the largest and most experienced helicopter sightseeing service in New York (25 years) is Liberty Helicopter, which flies out of the Westside Heliport (as well as the Downtown Manhattan Heliport), and has the best tours for your dollar. Liberty's six-passenger, red, white, and blue aircraft are extremely safe; in fact, Liberty has been incident-free since its first flights took off in 1985—important when your family is aboard.

Liberty is open year-round from 9 A.M. to 9 P.M. (including all holidays), so your kids can get a bird's-eye view of the dazzling skyscrapers any time of the day or night, in any season (reservations required). The skyline by night seems to appeal to adults more than kids, so try to pick a clear day for your trip, and arrive early so your children can spend some time at the heliport's windows watching the stream of helicopters glide onto the riverside tarmac. You can also go outside, walk south around the trailer complex, and stand along the storm fence feeling the propellers buffeting the air as the whirlybirds make their vertical ascents.

I recommend the Big Apple flight package (check website for current price), which covers approximately 14 miles, or about 20 minutes of total copter experience from climbing aboard and strapping in, to taking off, touring, and touchdown. If that sounds quick, consider that every minute is chock-full of high-flying excitement and unforgettable sights. You'll climb above the Hudson River, stare straight into the eyes of the Big Green Lady, then cruise up the river to the George Washington Bridge, passing midtown's magnificent skyscrapers and looping back to the heliport.

It's pricey, for sure. But if you want my advice, save the $600 you'd pay Magnifico the Magician for birthday party entertainment, and take your son or daughter with two best friends to Liberty Helicopter instead. Like me, they'll be talking about it for decades, and you'll be awarded Parent of the Year.

Cool Kid's Corner

If you're the birthday boy or girl (or even if you're not), ask for one of the double seats in the cockpit next to the uniformed pilot. You'll get a close-up look as he maneuvers the aircraft with a gazillion buttons and switches, and you'll peer down through your legs out the copter's glass nose. You can really feel the G-forces of the banking curves when you're sitting up front. Hold on tight . . . and I mean it!

little shop of crafts

❊ *Address: 431 East 73rd Street between York and 1st Avenues / 711 Amsterdam Avenue at the corner of 94th Street*

Phone: 212-717-6636; 212-531-2723

Ideal Age Group: 3 to 12

Admission: From $12.95 to $30; average is $20 for most craft projects

Website: www.littleshopny.com

The scene: a rainy autumn Saturday, your seven-year-old has just watched *Alvin and the Chipmunks* for the second time and appears to be rewinding for a third viewing, while your four-year-old is having a fit, kicking the kitchen cabinets out of frustration and boredom. The challenge: find something to do, quick!

In a spacious storefront on the Upper East Side (and a West side location with a café), the Little Shop of Crafts has been saving rainy days since 1992 with innovative, walk-in crafts for kids. While their pithy slogan is "Pick It, Paint It, Enjoy It," there's a lot more happening here than their motto suggests. Beading, mosaics, woodworking, T-shirt painting and, yes, plastercraft and pottery are on the long menu of make-it-yourself projects, along with the friendliest professional instruction in town.

Children, parents, and birthday party guests can select from hundreds of plastercraft figurines to decorate, from dolphins and dragons to cobras and cars. Plastercraft is cool because it can go home with your child the same day. Of course, there is no shortage of earthenware mugs, teacups, vases, napkin rings, piggy banks, cookie jars and candlesticks here either, but remember that pottery projects are different. The white bisque clay has already been fired once, and after your child paints, sponges or stencils on a personalized design, the object receives a final kiln-firing overnight. A couple of days later, you can pick up the finished piece—which can be a drawback if you're just visiting the city for the day or a short stay.

There are two trained artists at Little Shop at all times offering gentle guidance and encouragement, but they don't interfere with a child's masterpiece. Recently, I watched a nine-year-old from the nearby Ronald McDonald house (the cancer care center for children) paint a ceramic bowl that was a gift for his father back in Rhode Island. A calm and patient Little Shop artist sat with him throughout, making simple suggestions and boosting his confidence at a time when he really seemed to need it. This little boy was quite ill, but in that moment, he was happy.

The pre-cast crafts experience is repeated at **The Painted Pot** in Brooklyn (339 Smith Street, Carroll Gardens; 718-222-0334; www.paintedpot.com) where owner Lisa Meyer works hard to make art a positive family experience in her large, bright, relaxed space.

Cool Kid's Corner

The really special thing about Little Shop of Crafts (and unusual for crafts places like this) is that they don't rush you or your creativity because they don't charge for time, just for the piece you purchase. That means you can linger and lollygag as long as you like over your project, even come back the next day or the next week to finish it up. Isn't that cool? After all, no one would have told Michelangelo, "Hurry up, Mike!"

madame tussauds new york

❊ *Address: 234 West 42nd Street between 7th and 8th Avenues*

Phone: 212-512-9600

Ideal Age Group: 5 to 12

Admission: $37.93 adults / $30.35 children

Website: www.nycwax.com

Want to see Miley Cyrus *really* close up? Don't go to her concert or visit her website, head over to the Madame Tussauds—the amazing wax museum that's home to hundreds of the world's most famous folks. Every one of the nearly two hundred masterfully crafted wax figures looks so startlingly real, you'll find yourself doing constant double takes: Did Jennifer Aniston just blink; wasn't Wayne Gretzky standing over there a minute ago; did Tyra Banks just wave to us?

The original Madame Tussauds in London is perennially the city's most popular tourist attraction, but the marvelous, attention-grabbing $50 million museum on 42nd Street rivals it in appeal. The five-story physical structure alone is spectacular, with a glass-enclosed viewing platform suspended over the street, the only outdoor glass elevator in New York, and a giant hand reaching over the rooftop dangling the Madame Tussauds marquee from its fingertips.

It's the ornately decorated theme rooms inside, filled with all those uncanny wax portraits of famous actors, world leaders, sports stars and entertainment icons that will leave you drop-jawed in disbelief. Posing for photographs with your favorite celebrities and comparing physical attributes is a hoot. Who knew that Salma Hayek was this short, that Jodie

Foster's eyes were so electrifyingly blue, or that Brad Pitt wasn't as good-looking in person (or should I say, in wax)?

All these famous folks have been captured in precise detail by Madame Tussauds renowned wax artists. In fact, they take more than 250 measurements and photographs of each celebrity before starting the three-dimensional paraffin portraits, gathering information about hair texture, skin tone, eye color, even birthmarks and scars.

In a room called The Gallery, you'll see dozens of historical figures like Mahatma Gandhi, the Dalai Lama, Princess Diana, John F. Kennedy, and Nelson Mandela. Of course, it's the stars of sports and pop culture that so many kids come to see; people like Michael Jordan, Dwayne Johnson (formerly The Rock), Jon Bon Jovi, Oprah, Colin Farrell, Michael Jackson, The Beatles, Babe Ruth, and Beyoncé. In several other interactive exhibits, you can also hold hands with George Clooney at a romantic corner table, make Jennifer Lopez blush, pitch to Derek Jeter, or have your karaoke performance judged by *American Idol* host Simon Cowell. And, yes, I compared shoe size and stared up at Kareem Abdul-Jabbar's impossible height, just like all the other unbelievers.

Cool Kid's Corner

Check this out—the wax superstars have their hair washed, their make-up retouched and their jewelry polished almost daily. And can you guess what part of their bodies celebrities look at first when they see themselves in wax? The back—because it's the view they seldom get to see!

madison square garden tour

❋ *Address: 7th Avenue between 31st and*
   33rd Streets
   Phone: 212-465-5800
   Ideal Age Group: 5 to 14
   Admission: $17 adults / $12 children
   Website: www.thegarden.com

There is no sports fan like a New York sports fan, and they tend to raise little FAN-atics. If you've got one running around your house wearing a Knicks, Rangers or Liberty jersey, he or she is going to flip over this one hour, behind-the-scenes, all access tour of arguably the world's most famous sports arena—Madison Square Garden (MSG).

The fan fun begins when the energetic MSG tour guides appear at the waiting area in their snappy tour uniforms. First, you'll be ushered through a posh, season ticket holders' dining room where you view a short video history of the 40-year-old Garden (built in 1968, this is New York City's fourth Garden sports complex). Then, you're taken upstairs to one of the eighty-nine lavish skyboxes overlooking the arena, containing a dozen cushy seats, a kitchen, a bar, and closed-circuit TVs. These high-priced, private boxes are primarily, and not surprisingly, owned by large corporations to entertain business guests. You'll also see on-site venues like the WaMu Theater, and get a visit from an blue-and-orange-clad Knicks City Dancer—one of the athletic basketball cheerleaders.

The next stop is where kids go absolutely giddy: they're taken directly inside the Rangers, Knicks or Liberty locker rooms (which locker room depends on who has a game that night). Here, young fans see the actual players' lockers, their game uniforms, even some of the physical therapy tables where players get taped up before big games. This is a dream opportunity to take your photo with your favorite players' game jersey or gargantuan basketball shoes. One seven-year-old on our tour got to slip his foot into the size 21 sneaker of a New York Knick superstar. Later, a locker room attendant tossed the same ecstatic little boy an official NHL hockey puck—yes, he got to keep it.

The tour ends as you descend the stairs of this historic 20,000-seat arena to sit on the home bench of the Rangers or walk onto the court of the Knicks and Liberty, listening to amazing facts about the massive Garden scoreboard and how they turn a basketball court into a professional hockey rink—an amazing process that takes 20 hours. Our tour guide, an obsessed New York sports fan, finished up by challenging members of our group to a MSG-related sports trivia quiz. I didn't get one answer right—the seven-year-old kid knew them all.

Cool Kid's Corner

Take the last tour of the day if you want to increase your chances of bumping into one of your favorite Knicks, Rangers or Liberty players arriving before a game (the guide said it happens with regularity). Also look for the specially built Knicks locker room door that's a whole foot taller than any other doorway in the hall!

mars 2112

✲ *Address: 1633 Broadway at the corner of 51st Street*
Phone: 212-582-2112
Ideal Age: 4 to 12
Admission: Children's meals start at $10
Website: www.mars2112.com

When you're visiting another planet, it's always good to know a few words of the alien language, like *vabanu*, which means "hello" in Martian. Practice this with the accompanying three-fingered salute and you'll be ready for the best intergalactic dining experience of your earthly life.

No matter what language you speak or planet you call home, you're always welcome at Mars 2112—one of the most entertaining, family-oriented theme restaurants in New York City. If seeing the 25-foot flying saucer in the sunken plaza entrance doesn't convince you that you're in for an otherworldly adventure, perhaps stepping up to the departure gates in Mars 2112's futuristic lobby will.

After you enter, you're escorted onto a B-719 Ether Runner spaceship for the five-minute trip to the Red Planet. This 22-seat shuttlecraft is able to transcend the space-time continuum as it travels at warp speed, swaying, pitching, and bumping over Manhattan, past the *MIR* Space Station, and into a wormhole that catapults the ship towards Mars (all of which you watch from a really cool view port).

You arrive on Mars in the year 2112, where you're greeted by tech support crewmen convincingly dressed in blue-and-silver, *Star Trek*-like uniforms. You exit into the dim red interior of a subterranean crater with steaming lava pools underfoot and continue your extraterrestrial adventure. While you wait for your table (keep an eye on nearby video monitors for your number to pop up), you can visit the Mars Bar where parents can sip assorted mars'tinis and kids can enjoy a variety of non-alcoholic celestial concoctions.

The ultimate kid-pleaser (and time killer) is the Cyber-street Arcade, located in a red rock cave packed with 50 high-energy video and interactive games. From there you step through a narrow passage called the Rock Fissure into one of the two dining venues: the Crater's Edge, a 175-seat balcony area, or the cavernous Crystal Crater, which seats 325 people and includes a massive view-screen showing Martian landscape footage and scenes from Apollo missions. Be alert for a whacky visit from the wandering Mad Scientist.

Leafing through the Mars Times ("The Galaxy's Most Widely *Red* Martian Newspaper") you'll find a menu featuring space-age dishes like Quasar Quesadillas, Galactic Greek Salad, Supernova Spare Ribs, plus special kids' dishes like Pluto's Pasta and Crater Burgers. Unfortunately, theme restaurants are rarely known for their cuisine, and Martian food is no exception.

Cool Kid's Corners

Want to shake hands with a Martian? They appear daily at Mars 2112, an utterly silent species with snouts and rubbery blue and pink skin. You'll meet Captain Orion, Empress Gloriana, and a Martian baby, too—$QT\pi$ ("Cutie Pie" to earthlings). If you fall in love and want to take her home, you'll find doll-sized $QT\pi$s in the gift shop.

NBC studio tour and *today show* viewing

✳ *Address: 30 Rockefeller Plaza at West 49th Street between Fifth and Sixth Avenues*

Phone: 212-664-7174

Ideal Age Group: 7 to 14 (Children under 6 not admitted on tour)

Admission: $19 adults / $16 children / *Today Show* viewing is free

Website: www.nbcstore.com

Whenever my star-struck nieces and nephews visit me in the media capital of the world, the question they always ask is, "Will we see anybody famous?" Predictably, we spend a good portion of each day hunting for celebrities. Recent strategies include milling around the Ed Sullivan Theater during Letterman show tapings (5 P.M. at 1697 Broadway between West 53rd and 54th Streets), hanging out in the star-studded lobby of the Paramount Hotel (235 West 46th Street), or strolling through celebrity dense neighborhoods like the West Village or Madison Avenue near 60th Street.

There are two destinations that offer the highest probability of celebrity contact—the NBC Studio tour and the adjacent *Today Show* broadcast. The one-hour, guided NBC tour takes you into the bowels of the National Broadcasting Company, and it is especially fascinating for older kids held spellbound by the allure of TV. The tour departs from the NBC Experience Store by the main elevators and that's where so many "spottings" occur. Guests from shows like *Late Night with Conan O'Brien* and *Saturday Night Live*, as well as local news personalities, pass through the same halls and often ride the same elevators as tour guests.

Tour highlights include participation in a mock radio show underscoring NBC's origins in radio. I liked the "slap-and-crack" paddle used during radio sports broadcasts to mimic the sound of a bat hitting a baseball. You'll also get a peek into NBC's most famous studios (subject to availability), including *MSNBC* (home of Keith Olbermann and liberal brainiac Rachel Maddow) and *NBC Nightly News* as well as a visit to Studio 8H, the legendary home of *Saturday Night Live*. Then two members of your tour are selected to do a green-screen, mock weather report—I volunteered and forecast an August snowstorm for New York. Wrong.

If you can shake the kids out of bed early enough, you might also consider joining the crowd outside the *Today Show* studio. The live broadcast begins at 7 A.M. (until 11 A.M.) and if you arrive an hour early to get a front row position in the plaza, you'll not only stand nose-to-nose with Meredith Vieira, Matt Lauer, Ann Curry, and congenial weatherman Al Roker, you may even get to be on TV. Bring a cute baby, a birthday sign, or some other attention-getter and Al is sure to notice you during one of his brief weather spots.

Cool Kid's Corner

Here are some fun facts I learned on the studio tour: The NBC mascot is a peacock because the network was the nation's first to broadcast in color. And those three tones you sometimes hear during station identifications are the musical notes G, E, C—the initials for NBC's corporate parent, the General Electric Company.

new jersey children's museum

❄ *Address: 599 Valley Health Plaza; Paramus,*
  New Jersey
  Phone: 201-262-5151
  Ideal Age Group: 2 to 7
  Admission: $10 per person
  Website: www.njcm.com

"What do you want to be when you grow up?" It's a question that's often asked of kids, but it took a creative museum in New Jersey to realize that the answers could inspire an entire, multi-sensory play experience.

The New Jersey Children's Museum is a place for little people to pretend to be big people—playacting important grown-up jobs, dressing up in big people's uniforms, mimicking the words, gestures, and actions of parents, teachers, and the adults they admire. Here, your kids can enjoy a fun-filled afternoon as a surgeon, a ballerina, a firefighter, a helicopter pilot, a knight in armor (okay, not exactly a current career choice), a newscaster, an astronaut, an archaeologist, a construction worker, a boat captain, a postal worker, a chef . . . whew, I'll run out of space before this 15,000-square foot playpen runs out of ersatz professions!

The museum's converted warehouse location is both an exciting learning environment and a world of fantasy where kids are encouraged to touch and try everything. Do you have an aspiring hard hat in the house? The museum has a real backhoe in a nifty area that includes building blocks, construction toys, and cutaways of the warehouse structure itself so children can identify I-beams and cinder blocks. For future pilots, they've flown in an authentic Hughes 269 helicopter with its dome cockpit and dashboard dials intact. Your daughter the doctor can perform triage in an ambulance with working stethoscopes, surgical gowns, and X-rays hanging from a light box. Another popular destination is the mock grocery store complete with well-stocked shelves, kid-sized metal pushcarts, and a checkout register.

Of the more than 40 permanent exhibits, one of the best is a fully functioning television station, WKIDS, where children can watch themselves doing the news on two TV monitors. Then there is the ten-foot-tall Fantasy Castle with formidable turrets, a kids-only velvet throne room, and an assortment of medieval costuming to stage a Renaissance faire. Over at the horse stable, rodeo kids can ride stuffed stallions, while space travelers can use computer play stations in the 20-foot-high rocket ship. There's a new Driving and Drawing exhibit where children can create giant patterns on a 42-inch flat screen TV while using a steering wheel and gear shift to change colors and shapes. And for cyber fun, there's a virtual reality simulator that allows kids to stop a soccer ball in cyberspace, play drums by simply slapping their hands in the air, and listen as farm animals squeak, squawk, and squeal when touched in a virtual world. You'll even find New Jersey's largest kaleidoscope here—give it a spin and get psychedelic!

I realize that Paramus isn't one of the five boroughs. But since it's so close to the city, and doubles as a shopping mall Mecca, you have a great excuse to take your child to this perfect place for pretending.

Cool Kid's Corner

Climb aboard the real 1954 open-cab fire engine that's ready to roll. Turn on the red flashing lights, pull the yellow cord to clang the bell, and rush to a blaze in full fire gear. You drive, I'll pull the pumper hoses. Let's go!

new victory theater

※ *Address: 209 West 42nd Street between 7th and 8th Avenues*

Phone: 646-223-3010

Ideal Age Group: 4 to 14 (depends on show)

Admission: Show tickets are $10 to $35

Website: www.newvictory.org

The New Victory is Manhattan's oldest active theater—an intimate, elegant, 500-seat jewel box built by Oscar Hammerstein in 1900 that was lovingly restored to become New York City's first performing arts theater exclusively for children. Now, it's friendly façade beckons you to one of the great family treats on 42nd Street.

If you're from out of town and haven't been to this strip in a decade, you can toss out those images of 42nd Street as a seedy haven for X-rated movies houses and peep shops. Thanks to an independent, nonprofit organization called The New 42nd Street Inc., this historic block was revitalized and refurbished in the mid-1990s, and The New Victory became its first crowning achievement, followed by The New Amsterdam Theater (the *Mary Poppins* venue), **Madame Tussauds** (page 59), **Ripley's Believe It or Not!** Museum (page 87) and other stellar attractions for kids.

In this ornate, double-balconied auditorium—decorated in deep reds and gold, with eight pairs of chubby cherubs dangling their feet from the rim of a splendid central dome—young people are treated to a dozen dazzling productions of innovative new shows and celebrated classics every season. And make no mistake—this is not frivolous kiddie theater, unsuitable for the adults in tow. These are thoughtful, inspiring, and sometimes gritty or hilarious stage productions, professionally performed with astonishing sophistication.

Suddenly, great theater has been made accessible to kids in their very own playhouse.

The New Victory has assembled a magical mix of presentations from the elegant and awe-inspiring New Shanghai Circus to full-on flamenco from Spanish dance troupe Soledad Barrio & Noche Flamenca. There have been emotional dramatic plays, Bunraku-style puppetry, fabulous film festivals, and comedy acts, too, including the cutting-edge antics of England's Kneehigh Theatre—a favorite show that leaves the audience giggling contagiously. The complete schedule of seasonal programs is available on the website.

If there is any doubt that this handsomely restored theater has thoughtfully considered the entertainment needs of children, I'd like to point out one important detail: the theater is pitched more sharply than any I've ever seen. Which means that it's very easy for little heads to see over grandma's high-coifed hair.

Cool Kid's Corner

They rebuilt the Victory's grand exterior staircase so kids like you could race to the top before the show begins. Once inside, look closely at the end of each row of seats. See those carved bumble bees? They were put there long ago by a former Victory owner named David Belasco. Get it? BEE-lasco.

new york aquarium

✳ *Address: West 8th Street at Surf Avenue,*
Coney Island, Brooklyn
Phone: 718-265-3474
Ideal Age Group: 3 to 14
Admission: $13 adults / $9 Children ages 3–12 / under
3 years free
Website: www.nyaquarium.com

Sharks can smell prey a mile away, hear prey a half mile away, see prey 50 feet away, and taste prey as they chomp away! At the New York Aquarium, you can get almost close enough to these ferocious-looking, prehistoric predators to brush those multiple rows of razor sharp teeth.

Although the aquarium celebrates its 113th anniversary in 2009 (the oldest continually operating aquarium in the nation), this waterside home to sharks, stingrays, penguins, walruses, sea otters, and 8,000 other marine mammals and fish is nothing like the uninspired tank farm many of us remember from school outings as kids.

For one thing, the aquarium has the feeling of a natural habitat, in keeping with its Wildlife Conservation Society mission. The dramatic Sea Cliffs exhibit, for instance, is a three-hundred-foot rocky re-creation of a Pacific coastal habitat for sea otters, penguins, seals, and blubbery three-thousand-pound walruses. This is where you'll see the roly-poly toddler, Akituusaq—born in 2007, he's growing fast, gaining up to three walrus pounds a day!

Prepare to be splashed at the updated 1,600-seat Aquatheater with regular shows featuring the air-and-sea antics of barking sea lions and seals. Maybe I'm an easy audience, but to me there are few things as fascinating as watching those sleek brown swimmers snag herrings out of the air, spin in circles with the force of their fins, and perform synchronized somersaults with unparalleled grace.

The Explore the Shore exhibit features a Touch Tank filled with live sea stars, horseshoe crabs, and urchins, along with other hands-on marine exhibits. There's also the amazing Crash Wave Tank where you can live out your fantasy of being a barnacle. Every 30 seconds a man-made wave explodes overhead as you experience the unbelievable force of shoreline surf while remaining dry and unscathed.

The Alien Stingers exhibit is also a kiddie crowd-pleaser. The tanks of gelatinous jellyfish and phosphorescent sea life glow with stunning, iridescent color. Some of the creatures look like exploding fireworks, some like neon, some like they're internally lit with fiber optics.

Most kids want to dash off to the 90,000-gallon shark tank the moment they arrive. Standing with your nose inches away from the deadly teeth and beady eyes of circling behemoths like the 400-pound sandtiger will throw you and the kids into a delirious state of exhilaration and fear.

Cool Kid's Corner

Can you hold your breath as long as a seal? Can you stand the freezing cold of ocean life? You can answer these and other questions in the Sea Cliffs Exhibit. I held my breath for forty-five seconds (a seal can dive for twenty minutes), and the icy metal plate used to test skin for deep-water cold tolerance made me instantly shiver. I guess I'm no sea creature—it's a human's life for me!

new york city police museum

❄ *Address: 100 Old Slip between Water and*
   South Streets
   Phone: 212-480-3100
   Ideal Age: 5 to 14
   Admission: $7 adults / $5 children (suggested) / under
   2 years free
   Website: www.nycpolicemuseum.org

Popular shows like *CSI*, *Law and Order* and *The Closer* have topped the television ratings for years, elevating the image of crime fighters and making cops cool in the minds of the young and old alike. Parents and children can extend the police-appreciation experience at a downtown shrine to the men and women in blue—the New York City Police Museum.

Appropriately situated in the city's first precinct (lower Manhattan, where Gotham began), the museum occupies a landmarked police station built in 1909 and reassigned in 1998 to pay tribute to the world's largest police force. There are three floors of kid-friendly exhibits covering the long history of the NYPD since it's inception in 1845, capturing all of the real life drama of being a detective, street cop, bomb squad member, or special forces officer in a city where anything can happen and usually does.

The second floor is filled with a wild collection of lethal-looking police weapons and weird bad guy stuff. I liked the huge showcase of a gruesome but gripping assortment of gangster "rub out" paraphernalia like sawed-off shotguns, ice picks, cement blackjacks, and brass knuckles. There are lock picking tools once owned by the notorious bank robber Willie Sutton, a tommy gun used in gangland killings by Al Capone's henchmen, as well as an antique knife-gun (stab, then shoot?) and an array of cane handled pistols.

When I visited recently, a small school group was thrilled to crowd itself into an actual jail cell, complete with stainless steel toilet, a tiny sink, and double metal bunks. Nearby, kids were also taking their photos in an authentic mug shot line-up, but none of these pseudo thugs reached the six-foot mark. Some of the memorabilia is commonplace, but still cool—like early communications gear, hundreds of police shields from fallen officers, unusual whistles, and primitive handcuffs. On the first floor, there are two shiny police motorcycles, including a classic 1952 Indian bike, as well as a perfectly restored 1972 Plymouth Fury patrol car (painted black and green, and not the familiar blue and white). On the wall near the police car is a popular "siren sampler"—you push the colored buttons to blast one of six siren sounds and fill the space with urgency. Another must see is the 911 Remembered exhibit on the third floor—a moving, child-appropriate tribute to a terrible day. Be prepared for Ground Zero footage, photographs, and preserved artifacts that bear witness to the destruction as well as the heroism of the police officers who served that day.

Cool Kid's Corner

The first peacekeepers in New York City date back to the late 1600s when a nine-man patrol walked the streets in an effort "to pursue, attack, and capture pirates, vagabonds, and robbers." These watchmen carried green lanterns that they'd use to signal danger and call for help. Amazingly, the green globe lamps that appear on either side of the main entrance of every precinct house in the city today are a carryover from this three-hundred-year old practice.

new york doll hospital

❖ *Address: 787 Lexington Avenue between 61st and*
  62nd Streets
  Phone: 212-838-7527
  Ideal Age Group: 5 to 12
  Admission: Free (call ahead)

The doctor has been in since 1900 at this dedicated doll
hospital—the only one left in the United States. If that isn't
reason enough to take the kids, how do 100 upside-down
porcelain heads grab you? Or an equal number of spare torsos
hanging from the backroom rafters?

I'm going to tell you right up-front that the New York Doll
Hospital is a mess. Arms here, assorted legs over there, a pile
of wigs in the corner, boxes full of eyeballs in the back. You'll
probably be stunned by the chaos and clutter, but any child
who's ever left his toys lying around is going to love this place.

The 109-year-old doll hospital is not only an international
institution, it's the last survivor of a dead art. It's also incredibly
weird (and small, too, so they ask you not to bring school
groups). Broken, battered, and bruised dolls of every size,
shape, and pedigree are admitted here—and that's because
proprietor Irving Chais is probably the finest doll doctor in
the world.

Irving's grandfather started the hospital and it's been in the
family ever since. Irving grew up restringing dislocated arms,
repairing torn dresses, and re-gluing hair pulled out from years
of being loved (or run over by a car or chewed by aggressive
pets). Today, the world's most respected doll manufacturers
send him their repairs, and private collectors from as far as
South Africa and Australia trust only Irving to treat their valuable
Shirley Temples. He still works six days a week saving the lives
of treasured dolls, puppets and teddy bears, assisted by his

triage team: an equally dedicated doctor from Colombia, a dressmaker who's been with him for 45 years, and his daughter who specializes in wig reconstruction.

Sometimes Irving has to play psychiatrist, too. He says parents often come in asking him to make a copy of a child's beloved doll or teddy bear. But Irving suggests cleaning and restoring, rather than remaking, because it's the feeling of a doll, its smell, or the way its hair hangs, which children know so intimately. Change too many of those characteristics, Irving says, and children can become traumatized. Only a medical mensch like Irving would observe those vulnerabilities in a child's psyche.

Irving is constantly digging out original spare parts for the vinyl, rubber, tin, wood, plastic, porcelain, papier mâché, and clay dolls brought here for cleaning and repair. Besides his encyclopedic knowledge of dolls (he can identify, within seconds, the maker and country of origin of any doll you shove at him), Irving is also a funny man with some practiced one-liners. He's fond of saying that the hospital has never lost a patient, and that his medical malpractice costs are zero.

Cool Kid's Corner

Irving, who likes to play the grumpy old man, actually adores kids and will be thrilled to show you his kooky collection of body parts. Ask him to take you in back to see the hundreds of pairs of eerie glass eyes and the big box of creepy doll teeth. You're gonna love this guy, especially when he gurgles (go ahead, ask him).

new york hall of science

※ *Address: 47-01 111th Street, Flushing Meadows Corona Park, Queens*
Phone: 718-699-0005
Ideal Age Group: 4 to 12
Admission: $11 adults / $8 children (see website for free admission days)
Website: www.nyscience.org

There's no escaping it, when I was young I thought science stunk. Biology, physics, chemistry—it didn't matter, they all left me sleepy. Recess, on the other hand, was energizing and fun. Which leads me to believe that if you could combine recess and science class, you'd have a winning formula.

They've figured all that out at New York Hall of Science, where they have more than 400 spellbinding exhibits that are nothing like the boring, brain-drain experiments of my youth. Already ranked as one of the top ten science museums in the country, the Hall of Science got even better in 2007 with a 30,000-square-foot expansion of their outdoor Science Playground. And in the summer of 2009, a mini-golf course designed to teach the secrets of spaceflight opened in the cool Rocket Park.

There's cutting edge intrigue and gee-whiz thrills everywhere you look in the Hall. Activities are generally fast and easy to execute, so hyper kids can try a lot in a short time. Check out the Distorted Room where people go from midgets to mega-sized right before your eyes. The "Touch The Spring" illusion blew me away—I kept calling strangers over to grab the coil that wasn't there. The Antigravity Mirror was totally weird (look, I'm flying!), and you can also hunt for microbes and other little beasties in a drop of pond water under powerful video microscopes.

In the translucent north wing, visit the Sports Challenge, with its rock wall, a racecar reaction-time simulator, the wave-rider surfboard test, a fastball pitching cage, and other popular challenges that help explain the principles of physics. Don't miss Search For Life Beyond Earth, where you can drive a radio-controlled buggy around the surface of Mars, see how clouds form and spill rain, and smell space—that's right, they have actual rock and dust collected from an asteroid, and you can take a whiff. Finish off by standing on special scales that measure your body's water content—it bubbles up right before your eyes (all 9 gallons of me!).

The awesome Science Playground (the largest in the western hemisphere) is filled with outdoor educational contraptions that are wildly imaginative. High points include a 25-foot seesaw for school group teeter-tottering, a giant sun catcher exhibit using mirrors to aim sunbeams and hit targets, plus a new area dedicated to kids under six which includes a huge Lincoln Log-type timber climb.

Parent Note: Trying to decide between Liberty Science Center in New Jersey and the Hall? Choose the Hall. I am sorry to report that after a $100 million, two-year renovation, Liberty is a science experiment gone awry.

Cool Kid's Corner

There's a watery exhibit at the Hall of Science where you can make giant bubbles. Here's the same soapy formula they use at the Hall so you can whip up some bubble juice at home: Put 2/3 cup of liquid dishwashing soap (Dawn or Joy are best) in 1 gallon of water. Add 1 table-spoon of glycerin and let the solution age for five days. Presto, bubble mania.

new york transit museum

❖ *Address: Corner of Boerum Place and Schermerhorn Street, Brooklyn*
Phone: 718-694-1600
Ideal Age Group: 4 to 14
Admission: $5 adults / $3 children
Website: www.mta.nyc.ny.us/museum

During one of my first excursions into Manhattan, I begged my parents to take me on the subway. I was fascinated with the underground train, the simple novelty of holding my own token (remember those?) and dropping it in the turnstile. But when the subway finally rolled into the station, the deafening noise rattled my untrained ears and I freaked out. Luckily, I can now ride the IRT without parents in tow.

Today when out-of-town friends visit, their children often ask to ride the subway. So we do. We walk up to the front of the first car where we watch the signal lights changing in sequence and the spooky black of the subway tunnel racing by.

But I've discovered an even better place for a con centrated dose of subway sensations—the New York Transit Museum. The first hint that this is unlike any museum you've ever seen is its location in an authentic decommissioned IND station in Brooklyn Heights, built in 1936. For less than the price of two subway rides, children can pass through the turnstiles into this subterranean shrine to commuting—the largest museum in the country devoted to urban public transportation.

If you think about it, the subway is an incredible achievement—hundreds of miles of track dug through rock, dirt and mud by 30,000 men using not much more than picks, shovels, and strong immigrant backs. This amazing construction feat is well documented at the Transit Museum, where you can hear stories about diggers sucked out of underground tunnels and blown into the air. The popular Steel, Stone, and Backbone exhibit recounts in particularly gripping detail the building of the city's 100-year-old subway system. But the major attraction here is downstairs in the tube (with its still live, 600-watt third rail), the home of 19 restored subway cars, dating from as far back as 1904 (when a token was five cents). Kids can ring the bells on wooden cars with wicker seats, or pretend to be traveling to the 1939 World's Fair on cars painted in the official blue and orange exposition colors (the Mets didn't exist then).

They have some aboveground mass transit vehicles here too, including the sawed-off cabs from a pair of real New York City buses. Kids clamber up into the driver's seats behind huge steering wheels to peer through the classic fishbowl windows. On the newer bus, I was able to push the overhead route destination buttons with a satisfying high-pitched beep. You'll find original MTA conductor badges for sale in the gift shop along with other authentic subway memorabilia from the retired Redbird subway fleet. The museum also has the best collection of children's train books ever gathered in one place.

Cool Kid's Corner

Before they had subways in Brooklyn, horses pulled passenger trolleys along tracks. These fast-moving "horse cars" were dangerous to passing pedestrians who often had to leap out of the way, earning Brooklyn residents the name "dodgers." You guessed it—that's what they called Brooklyn's only professional baseball team until 1958, when they became the Los Angeles Dodgers.

new york waterway sightseeing cruises

❊ *Address: Pier 78 at West 38th Street on the Hudson River*

Phone: 800-533-3779

Ideal Age Group: 5 to 12

Admission: $26 adults / $15 children

Website: www.nywaterway.com

Circumnavigating the city by boat is a must-do attraction for many out-of-town families visiting New York. Almost the moment they arrive, they head directly to the Hudson River terminals to get a water view of this gigantic theme park before immersing kids in land bound adventures.

I must post a warning. The oldest and best known of the circle-the-city cruise lines offers a three-hour tour that could have been masterminded by Gilligan for the way it leaves children stranded. Three hours is an awfully long time when you're little. But one cruise line—New York Waterway—seems to understand the tolerance level of five- to twelve-year-olds, and has created an excursion that abbreviates the trip to a kid-manageable 90 minutes. You won't completely circle Manhattan Island, but you'll enjoy all the highlights children want to see—the Empire State Building, the Statue of Liberty, South Street Seaport, the United Nations complex, and the Brooklyn Bridge. You'll also loop around the southern tip of Manhattan for a unique perspective on the Ground Zero site and new Freedom Tower construction.

New York Waterway offers a free shuttle bus service for families staying in the midtown area that travels east and west on 57th, 50th, 42nd, and 34th Streets and conveniently drops you off at their sightseeing terminal at West 38th Street—just hail the red, white and blue buses as you would a cab. Once at the terminal, you'll find a number of clean, comfortable, modern ferries, part of the largest ferry and excursion fleet in the city. As the high-speed boat departs, take a seat on the left side of the upper deck (outside deck if it's sunny) for the best views of the passing skyline.

Knowledgeable and friendly guides pack a lot of fascinating city history into the water tour, with just enough silly trivia to hold a child's interest. I like this cruise for another reason: a lot of tourists feel compelled to take their kids to the Statue of Liberty, but, frankly, I think it's a destination that parents think kids should like, but few children actually do. The lines for both the Liberty Island Ferry and to climb the statue stairs are unbearably long, and you can consume an entire afternoon dragging a child around who's growing justifiably agitated. Many kids are content to see the Green Lady up close from the decks of a New York Waterway cruise, without stretching the limits of their fidgetiness on the crowded shores of Liberty Island.

Cool Kid's Corner

Here's some of that silly trivia I was telling you about: Did you know that if you take a Hudson River pier number and subtract 40, you can tell what street you're on? Or that the district name, Tribeca, stands for "triangle below Canal Street?" Or that the Brooklyn Bridge was built in 1883—ten years before cars were even invented? I learned a lot on my NY Waterway cruise.

panorama of the city of new york

※ *Address: Queens Museum of Art, Flushing*
  Meadows Corona Park, Queens
  Phone: 718-592-9700
  Ideal Age Group: 7 to 14
  Admission: $5 adults / $2.50 children
  Website: www.queensmuseum.org

Imagine taking the entire City of New York—all five boroughs, every one of the 895,000 buildings, the parks, the rivers, the airports, the 35 major bridges—and shrinking it down to fit inside one big room. That's exactly what they did to create the Panorama of the City of New York—the world's largest three-dimensional scale model, and an exact replica of Gotham.

The Panorama is simply so awesome that any child who has ever labored over a Legos creation approaches it with dropped jaw and wide eyes. It took 200 model makers, engineers, and draftsmen three years to build the Panorama, originally constructed as an exhibit for the 1964–65 World's Fair. The cityscape was updated in 1994 by the original builders (Lester & Associates) to include 60,000 changes and additions—so if you live in this city there's a good chance that it includes your apartment building.

During the World's Fair, 1,400 visitors a day viewed the expanse from tracked cars (one of which is on display) that simulated helicopter flight at heights of 3,000 to 20,000 feet. Now you walk along an elevated ramp with glass floors that traces the perimeter of the 9,335-square-foot model. One of the Panorama's best features, which always elicits delight from young visitors, is the night scene enhancement. Every few minutes the room lights dim and the city glows with 2,500 green, orange, red, and blue lights, augmented with special black light illumination. The entire effect is totally eerie and wonderful.

The first thing city kids will want to do is find their home or school, along with landmarks like Yankee Stadium, the Empire State Building (just 15 inches tall at this one-inch to 100-foot scale), and the Statue of Liberty (look below your feet along the west walkway). If you want an improved view, bring along some binoculars—it's worth it. In 2008, the Queens Museum also introduced a 12-minute short film featuring archival footage of the making of the Panorama and it's a kid-worthy attraction.

You might be wondering if the World Trade Center Towers are still part of the Panorama. Yes, they are. At least until the new Freedom Tower and surrounding buildings are erected at Ground Zero in the years ahead, when those will find their way into this magnificent model, too.

Cool Kid's Corner

There are three great things to look for while you're here: the miniature airplanes taking off and landing at La Guardia airport—see if you can follow them flying across the black night sky of the ceiling; an enormous elevator, once the world's largest, located in the lobby of the building that was used to carry World's Fair tourists; and the cool New York Story pop-up toy in the gift shop that allows you to hold Manhattan in the palm of your hand.

the real world

✳ *Address: North End of Rockefeller Park at Chambers Street on the Hudson River*

Ideal Age Group: 2 to 10

Admission: Free

Tom Otterness is the kind of artist who creates like a child. His imagination is utterly fresh and nimble, and there is an enthusiasm and playfulness in everything he does. I imagine that to him the world of fantasy is comfortable and real, while reality seems ridiculous.

Perhaps this is why his Real World playground of absurd and comical creatures in Hudson River Park speaks the visual language of children so perfectly. It is impossible to dislike Otterness' fairy-tale family of pint-sized busy bodies—a civilization of bronze smiley faces I call the "Pill Box" men (because of those hats). Swimming in a sea of oversized pennies—the artist's reference to the nearby Financial Center—these and all sorts of half-human, half-animal carnivalesque sculptures delight children of every age in their riverfront tiny town.

Otterness is a Kansas native (possible Oz influence here) whose highly recognizable, bulbous sculptures have been commissioned for projects throughout the city, including an underworld creation for the Mass Transit Authority (his light-hearted sculptures, including the ever chomping "alligator in the sewer," completely inhabit the 14th Street/8th Avenue station). He likes to make public art because it reaches so many people. He works in bronze because he says it gets polished when people touch it—that way he can tell which of his sculptures children love most. His genial Dodo bird is the frequently nuzzled playmate of countless toddlers just a few hundred yards away in the **Rockefeller Playground** (page 89).

He's created so many crazy characters in his Real World parklet, doing so many offbeat things, your eyes will have to work overtime. At the south entrance, you'll spot a bulldog chained to a water fountain, barking at a cat, who's watching a bird, who's eyeing a worm. Over there is Humpty Dumpty on the violin. Nearby, two frogs are wrestling under a penny fountain, while another rests on a lily pad. And everywhere the Pill Box men are making mischief.

You'll discover that the Real World is particularly well suited to young children learning their numbers. There's a long winding Penny Path snaking through the entire sculpture garden with an alternating little feet motif. Children can step on the feet while counting pennies along the walkway (shoes and socks off is best) for a game that fully engages little minds and bodies.

Note: If you have a little extra time, walk north on the river promenade about three hundred yards to the newly reconstructed **Pier 25** (between Franklin and N. Moore Streets). There you'll find a miniature golf course, beach volleyball, a beautiful new playground and fields, river overlooks, historic boats, and kid's outdoor movies on summer evenings.

Cool Kid's Corner

Mr. Otterness has tucked some of his most magical sculptures in hard-to-see places. Can you find the cigar-smoking turtle on the wall, the dark monk with a sickle sitting atop a light post, the gagged cat, the unplugged phone, and the man-snake reading on the pole? The first one to find all five wins!

ripley's believe it or not!

- *Address: 234 West 42nd Street between 7th and 8th Avenues*
  Phone: 212-398-3133
  Ideal Age Group: 4 to 14
  Admission: $26.95 adults / $19.95 children ages 4 to 12
  Website: www.ripleysnewyork.com

While YouTube may be every kid's online source for odd and outrageous thrills, there is one place in New York City that trumps all others for concentrated weirdness—Ripley's Believe It or Not!

I have never met a child (or an adult for that matter) who doesn't love a startling dose of strange, kooky, and creepy stuff—and Ripley's has the most curious collection ever assembled. Here's a short sampling: the stuffed carcass of a two-headed calf, 24 authentic shrunken heads (the world's largest collection of shriveled noggins from the Jivaro Indians of Ecuador), a 2,500-year-old mummified Egyptian hand, the stomach contents of a great white shark (an anchor, shovel, and shoes are among the edibles), and a four-legged chicken purportedly bred by a Romanian farmer to yield more drumsticks. If those oddities don't evoke an avalanche of "No way!" and "Awesome!" exclamations from your children, keep moving, because there's 17,000 square feet of similarly inexplicable, one-of-a-kind attractions at Ripley's.

LeRoy "Robert" Ripley came to New York in 1913 as a sports cartoonist, but got more attention for his illustrated, syndicated feature on amazing achievements. The man who coined the phrase "truth can be stranger than fiction," then spent the rest of his life spanning the globe collecting the most unbelievable and grossest stuff he could find. He opened his first Ripley's Believe It or Not! museum in Times Square in 1939 (the last one closed in 1972, reopening most recently in 2007), when it was known for "curioddities" from over 200 countries.

Need a few more enticements to this museum of amazement and awe? How about a lock of hair cut from Abraham Lincoln's lethal head wound (along with rare strands from Elvis Presley, John F. Kennedy, and George Washington), a fossilized walrus penis used as a fighting club (don't worry, it's harmless and G-rated), a wax figure of Robert Wadlow, an 8'11" anomaly of nature who was the tallest man in modern history, a stuffed six-legged cow, a replica of the Burmese Padaung tribeswoman (known for stretching their necks to extreme lengths using brass rings), and a collection of more than 20,000 four-leaf clovers.

There's a fair amount of freak show memorabilia here and lots of photos of malformed humanity that some parents might find impolitic (the astonishing acrobat with no lower body, the world's ugliest woman, an armless man with incredibly dexterous feet), but the bulk of the exhibits are kid-rated, fascinating, and fun. Believe it.

Cool Kid's Corner

Okay, call me sick, but I was mesmerized by video images of human impalements, including a crazy scene of two men riding tandem on a motorcycle, both skewered through the chest by a flying pipe from the back of a stopping truck—and they both survived! You also have to try the black-hole tunnel attraction. I won't say more, just be prepared for a wacko walk that's both disorienting and little stomach churning—be glad you're not on a diet of anchors, shovels, and shoes!

rockefeller playground

※ *Address: Rockefeller Park, Vesey Street on the Hudson River*

Ideal Age Group: 2 to 10

Admission: Free

Website: www.bpcparks.org

I was a light, wiry, nimble kid who loved to climb the maples and dogwoods in my suburban neighborhood. I could shimmy 30 feet off the ground in seconds. Unfortunately, a good climbing tree is hard to find in the city, which is why I suggest that children practice their vertical scampering at the Rockefeller Playground. I'm tempted to call this the city's best playground not only because it's an excellent place to climb, jump, run, crawl, slide, skip, tumble, dig, push, wriggle, ride, leap, hang and hop—but because of its idyllic setting.

This masterfully designed playground (by award-winning landscape architect Sonja Johansson) sits on seven acres of continuous parks and gardens just steps from the Hudson. In this open, airy environment, children can bask in sunlight and sea breeze, features that contribute to an expansive play experience. In a city where children are too often confined to small, limited play spaces, Rockefeller Playground lets kids know they're free to go wild. And they do.

Designed to be more challenging for kids as they go from the north to south end, to my eye the playground is also built as a microcosm of the city—with a maze of "high-rise" structures, bridges, and towers looking down on the bustling activity of ground level play areas, hopscotch games, and sandboxes. This playground is also extremely safe, so parents find they can temporarily relax, have a chat, and just let kids play.

Opportunities abound for that. At the south end is a cheerful red carousel for smaller children that parents can push or kids can pedal power. It travels slowly on its own circular track and always prompts a passing parade of smiling faces. Further on is a wooden-bowed bridge (run fast, make lots of banging sounds with your feet), sliding poles, a bright yellow spiral slide, a three-foot elevated sandbox for standing play, lots of swings, muscle-building climbing nets, and several springy jumping platforms. The expansive climbing area is clearly marked (AGES 9 AND OLDER, AGES 2 TO 5, etc.), so that parents can match apparatus difficulty to a child's skill level. Bring your chalk—the entire playground is covered with a thick, black, spongy surface that not only cushions inevitable falls, it's perfect for chalk drawings and hopscotch boards.

If you find yourself uptown, visit two other popular playgrounds in Central Park near Fifth Avenue, one at **68th Street** (look for the rough hewn gazebo and tree houses) and the other at **72nd Street** (tremendous sand play areas and concrete tunnels). In Brooklyn, I like **Harmony/9th Street Playground** with structures that make musical notes, an oversized playable xylophone, along with cool tunnels and elevated chain bridges (Prospect Park at 9th Street, www.prospectpark.org).

Cool Kid's Corner

Check out **Teardrop Park** (River Terrace between Murray and Warren Streets), the bonus play area just a scooter ride away from Rockefeller Playground. It's two acres of simple fun tucked between a couple residential buildings, which you'll love because it has the single best slide in the city—a 35-foot slippery slope with a long steel landing strip to deposit you safely into soft sand. You can climb back to the top along a rock-hopping incline that's as awesome as the slide.

roosevelt island aerial tram

❄ *Address: 59th Street and 2nd Avenue*

Phone: 212-832-4543

Ideal Age Group: 3 to 10

Admission: $4 round-trip per person (MetroCard accessible)

Website: www.rioc.com

In 2002, the popular comic book hero Spider-Man leapt onto the big screen for the first time, turning a New York City landmark into one of the film's biggest stars. In the movie's climactic scene, the Green Goblin throws Mary Jane Watson off the Queensborough Bridge, and the web-slinger has to decide whether to save his secret sweetheart or rescue horrified passengers trapped on the adjacent Roosevelt Island tram.

You can watch the DVD to recall what happens next, but if you want to experience the midair excitement in person (without the cable-dangling terror, of course) head over to 59th Street on the east side, where every 15 minutes the aerial tramway starts its four and a half minute glide, 250 feet above the river on huge cables. If you think the tram is just a practical, if not picturesque way to commute between the Roosevelt Island and Manhattan, you're not thinking like a child. To a kid, this is a carnival ride, a bubble in the sky, a great way to fly!

The large, four-sided glass cabins, carrying up to 125 passengers at a time, offer an amazing view of the towering skyscrapers of midtown. There are a thousand things to see when you're way up high, and children don't miss a thing: the multicolored specks of cars and taxis racing down the black ribbons of the avenues, chubby tugboats pushing barges through the swirling river waters below, helicopters taking off from the 63rd Street Heliport, a building fire trailing smoke somewhere far off in Brooklyn.

After the aerial sightseeing tour is over, the tram follows a steep slope to its docking descent and jerks to rest with a few bumps that always amuse little ones. Once off the cable car, walk your children over to the big window of the tram's engine room. You can peek inside to see the enormous yellow gears and the blue, orange, and green tinker toy interior. Was this place made for kids or what?

Don't quit now. This is a fun-filled little island that starts with a 25¢ ride on the red minibuses along Main Street. Get off at the northernmost stop where you and your children can continue to walk past the beautiful community gardens along the East River promenade heading to the child-sized, 50-foot stone lighthouse at the island's tip. There's a wonderful sun-filled park for picnicking here, away from the bustle of Manhattan. The native Canarsie Indians called this little island Minnahannock, loosely translated as "It's Nice to Be on the Island." Yeah, sure, but who would want to miss the return ride to Manhattan on the aerial tram?

Cool Kid's Corner

Here's my favorite thing to do on the tram. Watch for the other cable car passing by in the opposite direction. You'll meet at about midpoint where you can make friendly, funny faces at the huddled commuters floating by. And if you want to catch the Roosevelt Tram in its very first movie role, pick up a DVD of the 1981 film *Nighthawk*, with Sylvester Stallone. Nothing like watching those cable cars dangling by a few metal strands to heighten the excitement of your next tramway trip—but, hey, it's only a movie!

rose center for earth and space

❄ *Address: Central Park West at 81st Street*
Phone: 212-769-5200 for Space Show reservations
Ideal Age Group: 8 to 14
Admission: $15 adults / $8.50 children (suggested)/or
with Space Show admission $24 adults and $14 children
(ages 2–12)
Website: www.amnh.org/rose

The gleaming cube of glass is so bright and breathtaking, and the four million pound Hayden Sphere hovering inside it is so massive and magnificent, you just know the Rose Center for Earth and Space is going to be extraordinary, sensational, and spectacular. And you're never disappointed.

The Rose Center is part of the **American Museum of Natural History** (page 21), and your ticket to the museum gains you access to this updated center. I've included it as a separate *50 Best* location not only because the scope of the astronomical science here stands alone, but also because it's ill-advised to hustle children through both exhibition-rich venues in a single day. You're not only going to miss a lot of good stuff, you'll have some tired and irritable kids in tow.

I started my afternoon tagging along behind a group of sixth-grade science students, watching an engrossing short film about black holes. We learned why they call these matter-sucking celestial bodies "gravity's ultimate triumph," and tensed when the narrator said we'd reached "the edge of no return." Yipes!

The Gottesman Hall of Planet Earth includes the world's oldest known rock as well as the Earth Event Wall with television broadcasts on global earthquakes and volcanoes as they happen. You can even create your own mini-earthquake by jumping on a bull's-eye painted on the floor and measuring your impact on the seismometer needle nearby.

The Heilbrunn Cosmic Pathway, a gently sloping 360-foot walkway that orbits the Hayden Sphere, leads you on an exploration of 13 billion years of cosmic evolution. Want to feel small? While it looks like a mere half-dollar when spied from the floor of the pathway, the Sun is actually so big you could fit one million planet Earths inside of it!

The Hayden Planetarium is where the Rose Center's most out-of-this-world attractions happen. The current multi-sensory space show, Cosmic Collisions, narrated by Robert Redford, uses the world's most powerful virtual reality simulator to catapult you into outer space where ginormous explosions shaped our solar system. In the nearby Big Bang Theater, an equally dramatic presentation by Maya Angelou explains how the entire universe materialized from a point of energy smaller than a grain of sand (try thinking about that without overloading your mental microprocessors). And for really far out entertainment, visit on Friday and Saturday nights for SonicVision, featuring mind-bending digital animation set to the music of Moby, U2, and others pop artists.

Cool Kid's Corner

If you're feeling chubby, just step on the lunar scale and see how ultra-light you'd be on the moon. Digital scales embedded in the floor of the Cullman Hall of the Universe will also reveal your weight on Saturn, Jupiter, a neutron star, and the Sun. No need to lose weight, just travel to the stars . . . at the Rose Center.

socrates sculpture park

❖ *Address: 32-01 Vernon Boulevard at Broadway,*
Long Island City, Queens
Phone: 718-956-1819
Ideal Age Group: 3 to 14
Admission: Free
Website: www.socratessculpturepark.org

Too much art in too many pretentious settings can discourage a kid. I had the misfortune of plunking myself down on an enormous leather Claus Oldenburg baseball mitt at the Guggenheim once, and was soundly chastised by a passing museum guard (she actually called me a "dummy"). Hey, I couldn't help it, the impulse just came over me.

No such problem for energetic souls at the Socrates Sculpture Park. Children of all ages can touch, hang from, climb over, sit on, and fully explore dozens of large-scale sculptures in this four and a half-acre waterfront park, which is open every day of the year. The inspiration of Queens steel girder sculptor, Mark di Suvero, this unassuming sculpture garden was an illegal garbage dump for years, until it was reclaimed and revitalized by the artist and his neighbors in 1986.

Not that Socrates Sculpture Park has forgotten its humble beginnings. You can occasionally find a piece of rusted wire here or the remnants of old sheet metal in the bushes over there. But, in general, the former rubble strewn lot offers a kind of rugged sanctuary from the oily garages, welding shops, and masonry warehouses that still survive on nearby Vernon Boulevard. It's okay to run, play, throw a ball, or picnic in the shadow of Socrates' towering wood, stone, and steel creations by both well-known and emerging artists. It's a particularly smart excursion with children on hot days when the East River breezes cool off the shoreline.

Feeling climby? Many of the sprawling sculptures have dimensions and surfaces that are made for acrobatic types and rival the best outdoor playground apparatus (but be careful, as there are no cushioned surfaces below). Another favorite pastime for children here is locating their initials in the granite alphabet wall that borders the park on the east side. Exhibits change with regularity, so there's always something new looming before you. And for offbeat art-making, the park offers free drop-in workshops from 12 to 3 P.M. on Saturdays during the spring, summer, and fall. They have a cool Summer Solstice Celebration and Halloween Harvest Festival geared for kids, too. Check the website.

Cool Kid's Corner

Socrates is not just cool because it's located right on the river, with awesome views of Manhattan. You're going to love this place for another reason—you'll have a chance to meet lots of imaginative artists working on-site. They won't be using delicate paintbrushes, wearing berets, or making art in quiet studios either. These sculptors create their amazing, massive pieces out-doors, wearing industrial coveralls, using rock-crushing jackhammers, and white-hot welding torches. These same dynamic artists lead the Saturday workshops, so get ready to participate in art-making like you've never seen it before.

sony wonder
technology lab

❉ *Address: 550 Madison Avenue at 56th Street*
   Phone: 212-833-8100
   Ideal Age Group: 6 to 14
   Admission: Free (Avoid lines by calling at least one week
   ahead for advanced reservations, 212-833-5414)
   Website: www.sonywondertechlab.com

Open up your kid's brain and you might find a biomass of ones
and zeros—the binary code behind all things digital. Like it
our not, our children have technology in their blood, with
synapses that fire faster than ours ever did as well as a wizardry
for media multi-tasking.

At Sony Wonder Technology Lab (SWTL) they don't fight
this reality, they just keep their high-tech cyber station as
current as possible and let kids have fun while challenging
their mental microchips. In the fall of 2008, SWTL completed
an awesome renovation, giving children a chance to explore
the very latest in Sony's sophisticated robotics, eye-popping
communications technology and virtual gadgetry.

First, you're greeted by Sony Technology Guides, handed
a Sony Wonder identity card, and whisked up to a flashy
entrance hub with eight log-in stations. On-screen guides then
help you magnetically encode your ID card with your name,
image, voice imprint, favorite color, and music genre. The card
then becomes your pass for activating the exhibits (when the
camera locks onto your image, make a funny face for repeated
laughs every time you swipe the card).

Now you're free to descend the chrome and neon ramps
into three more floors of edutainment. Start by swiping in at the
Community Diagram to digitally pinpoint exactly where you are

at SWTL and locate your friends (kind of like a digital version of Harry Potter's Marauder's Map). On the oval Interactive Floor you move around in a pool of colored light and merge your color halo with other visitors to form crazy rainbows. In the Robot Zone, you get to control one of six robots equipped with light and touch sensors and work the controls to accomplish tricky tasks. Want to see if you're made for TV? At the HDTV Production Studio you and several friends can play the roles of director, camera operator, field reporter, and host, while taping an environmental news report. The entire broadcast is played back for your review . . . and big laughs.

An absolute favorite attraction is the Dance Motion Capture experience. You step inside the markerless motion capture booth, do your best dance steps or silly moves, then watch them mirrored back by your favorite Sony animated characters in digitized performances on huge display screens— totally and utterly amazing. Another popular destination at SWTL is In The Game, where three immersion alcoves are dedicated to the latest Playstation action games with their stunningly realistic, high-def graphics. Sony Wonder also has a 73-seat theater where they show sensational high-definition movies, as well as free children's screenings of popular feature films. Check the website for a schedule and to reserve seats.

Cool Kid's Corner

Don't leave SWTL without trying the Virtual Surgery experience. Using an ultra high-tech Haptic controller (like a joy stick that's alive), you perform open-heart surgery on a virtual patient. Freaky thing is, you can actually feel the surgical knife cutting through skin and tissue! Haptic technology is being used today to train surgeons . . . and it puts you smack dab in the middle of the operating room, too.

swedish cottage marionette theater

※ *Address: Central Park, enter at West 81st Street*
Phone: 212-988-9093
Ideal Age Group: 3 to 9
Admission: $8 adult, $5 children / reservations required;
check online for group and party rates
Website: www.centralparknyc.org

You walk through the woods, skip along a flower-edged pathway, then stumble upon a small wooden cottage nestled next to a beautiful garden. You climb a few steps, open the door, and look up to see dozens of silent marionettes hanging along exposed rafters—there's a princess over there, a wizard over your head, an Indian in feathered headdress suspended above the doorway. What sort of fantasy place is this? What kind of magic happens here?

You've discovered the charming Swedish Cottage Marionette Theater—a cozy place just a hundred yards walk from Central Park West that has introduced generations of New York children to the wonders of live puppet theater. Originally built in Sweden for the 1876 Centennial Fair in Philadelphia and later brought to New York, the peak-roofed, arch-windowed balsam fir structure served many functions before 1973, when it began to house puppet productions.

This sweet, kid-sized theater has rows of curved, low benches facing a gold-curtained stage. The colorful sets are marvelously elaborate and creative, the ornate marionettes (each a couple feet tall) are finely crafted and expressive, and the sophisticated puppet work here is deft, polished, and beautiful to watch. The cottage produces a new show every year (there's a two-week break in July and a one-month hiatus in September), always with an urban twist on a classic fairy tale such as Cinderella, Peter Pan, or Jack and the Beanstalk. Their version of Sleeping Beauty, for instance, had her royal family living in Central Park's Belvedere Castle and the African-American god-fairy singing gospel tunes and imparting wisdom laced with inner-city jargon. Brilliant.

Typically, there's an amusing, five-minute introduction from a member of the puppeteering crew, when he or she demonstrates the workings of a marionette and then asks audience members to help wake the puppets sleeping behind the curtain with a collective scream. The friendly and exceptionally patient puppeteers reappear after the show to answer questions. They seem well aware that these one-hour puppet performances could be a child's first exposure to theater of any kind, and they try hard to ensure a positive experience.

New York has other excellent puppet theaters for children. **PuppetWorks** (page 131) is locally famous for more than 25 years of traditional marionette productions at its storefront theater in Brooklyn's ultimate kid-friendly neighborhood, Park Slope.

Cool Kid's Corner

After a visit to the Swedish Cottage lots of kids want to create puppet shows of their own. If that's you, then visit **Dinosaur Hill** (306 East 9th Street at 2nd Avenue; 212-473-5850), a puppet palace with hundreds of hand and finger puppets, plus high-quality marionettes—unicorns, clowns, magicians and villains—made especially for kids, with color-coded strings that untangle in a jiffy.

TADA! youth theater

* *Address: 15 West 28th Street, 2nd floor, between Broadway and Fifth Avenues*
  Phone: 212-252-1619
  Ideal Age Group: 4 to 13
  Admission: Multi-week class sessions from $230–$375
  Website: www.tadatheater.com

This is a city for entertainers, with hundreds of Broadway plays, cabarets, staged readings, and musical concerts going up every night. Talented actors, singers, dancers, and performers of every size, shape, and vocal range are giving their all to make audiences laugh, cry, and shake with excitement. It's electrifying stuff, and if you're a little person growing up here you can't help but be affected; you've got to wonder if maybe, just maybe, there isn't a little bit of star in you.

Well, raise the curtain and turn on the footlights, because I know the perfect place to find out—TADA!. This unique theater company and performance school gives kids a place to develop their voice, dance, and stage techniques in a safe, supportive, upbeat environment. And TADA! is exclusively for children—in fact, it's New York's only youth theater ensemble, with classes that are relevant to kids, and shows on TADA!'s main stage that address preteen and teen issues.

Young performers from every ethnic and socioeconomic background come here to hone dramatic skills, learn improvisation, and play theater games. And as it turns out, many of the city's finest professional actors aren't waiting tables either, they're teaching at TADA!. Every after-school and Saturday class is taught by a choreographer/director and a musical director with a maximum of 20 children per class, so even the more introverted students get attention.

Each class and camp session ends with an exuberant performance at TADA! for families and friends (around here, all the world really is a stage). Many children in the musical theater school then try out in open auditions to become a member of TADA!'s ensemble troupe, which puts on three high-quality, original productions a year.

Watching a class of eight- to twelve-year-olds in TADA!'s rehearsal space, I was reminded of a humiliating experience I had in the third grade singing an "Edelweiss" solo in an all-school assembly. I thought I'd pulled it off quite well, but was later mocked by the music teacher for a few squeals on the high notes. End of singing career. You can be sure there's nothing like that going on at TADA!. The instructors I saw were positively thrilled with every sung note and dance step, and the kids all seemed to shine in the generous spotlight. I was also amazed at the camaraderie between these preteens, with the more confident kids pulling the wallflowers, well . . . off the wall.

Cool Kid's Corner

I thought you might like to hear part of a poem written by a kid like you who was excited to be performing at TADA, "I shouted, I screamed, I strutted, I pranced, did cartwheels and flips and sang and danced, for I had just gotten the best news so far, that I would belong to a place called, TADA!" Okay, so it doesn't really rhyme at the end, but it's still original, unique, avant-garde . . . it's showbiz!

tah-poozie

※ *Address: 50 Greenwich Avenue between 6th and 7th Avenues*
Phone: 212-647-0668
Ideal Age Group: 3 to 12
Admission: Free

Every New York City parent who has ever filled a goodie bag is beholden to former kibbutznik, Schmuel Kerhaus, and the endless variety of silly trinkets in his narrow Village store, Tah-Poozie.

This is simply the best party favor place on the planet, with all the groovy gewgaws and goofy gifts you'll ever need for any age group. And in a world of hundred-and-fifty-dollar Playstations and hundred-dollar skateboards, Tah-Poozie also makes it easy for a city kid to find true toy satisfaction for just a few bucks (or a week's allowance).

Owner Shmuel Kerhaus has been lining the walls of his sliver-like shop with affordable fun since 1988, and he knows what makes children happy. Kids go absolutely wild here sifting through shelves upon colorful shelves of toys and games and gizmos, most priced from $1 to $10, and all thoughtfully placed near a child's eye level.

Shmuel gave me the total toy tour (say that three times fast), complete with his bubbly non-stop demonstrations, which kept us both laughing. He refills his display bins with the latest novelties almost weekly, so you'll see something new with every visit. Check out the hysterical Press Me Pigs, flashing star-shaped balls (yes, they bounce), tattoo Band-aids, assorted squirting insects, floating eyeballs, rainbow viewers, mini-mini colored pencil sets, and tiny animals that grow gigantic inside soda bottles.

You'll love the wild wind-up walkers (crabs move sideways, knights gallop, frogs hop), the Hand Blasters (safe, snapping gun powder balls), creepy Bone Chiller ice trays, and the Pick Your Nose cups that make it appear you have a toucan, chameleon, zebra, or shark's snout while you're sipping . . . very funny. Shmuel also has classics like that bathtub companion, Diver Dan, who's still kicking his flippers after all these years, a childhood favorite of mine called Magic Rocks, along with spy glasses to see who's sneaking up behind you or a pocket-sized periscope to snoop around corners. Each one is a guest giveaway they'll never forget, so for a doozy of a birthday party, get over to Tah-Poozie.

Since you're in the neighborhood, consider two other quick stops: the **Firestore** (page 121) just down the street, and a few blocks uptown visit the excellent children's gift shop, **Kidding Around** (60 West 15th Street, 212-645-6337, www. kiddingaround.us). Consistently rated one of the best in the city, you'll find top quality children's playthings here, without the crushing crowds or the impersonal personnel at the mega stores. At Kidding Around they always seem to suggest the right combination of plush toys and puppets, building blocks and books, miniature cars and construction toys, baby shower gifts and games.

Cool Kid's Corner

At Tah-Poozie they have an awesome collection of flip-books with samples of zippy scenes for you to try before you buy. I was mesmerized by Shark Bite (chomp!), Stunt Auto (crash!), The Cat and the Butterfly (swipe! swat!), Jumping Dolphin (swish!), and the History of Flight (wheee!). Did you know that this is exactly how films are made? One picture frame at a time, moving quickly past your eyes.

tannen's magic

Address: 45 West 34th Street between Fifth and Sixth Avenues, Suite 608
Phone: 212-929-4500
Ideal Age Group: 5 to 14
Admission: Free
Website: www.tannenmagic.com

Hocus Pocus! Abracadabra! Simsalabim! These are the magic words. Children all over the world learn them almost as soon as they can talk, and every time the words are spoken there's the anticipation of something fantastic about to happen, something amazing and wonderful.

As it turns out, the world's epicenter for constant quakes of magical excitement is right here in New York at Tannen's Magic. The most famous magic shop on the planet—with more than 12,000 tricks and illusions in stock—has been a Mecca for amateur and professional magicians for more than 75 years. New Jersey native, David Copperfield, got his start at Tannen's purchasing card tricks as a teenager. Siegfried and Roy bought their first illusions from Tannen's founder, Lou Tannen, 30 years ago. Dick Cavett, a master at sleight of hand, is a regular customer, and so is the brilliant street magician and endurance artist, David Blaine. Even Muhammed Ali, a magic nut, has shopped here.

The store is filled, floor to ceiling, with the countless colorful props that make every magic show so unforgettable—silk scarves, magic wands, shiny coins, mysterious black boxes, startling straitjackets, razor sharp swords, dangling ropes, and decks upon decks of rigged playing cards. And the best part is, everyone behind the counter at Tannen's knows how to use this stuff.

new york's 50 best places to take children

That means you get to see a live show every minute, because their counter staff of professional magicians is always eager to perform a close-up sleight or mental effect. During the daytime, Tannen's is also a hangout for the brother-and-sisterhood of magicians who make frequent pilgrimages here to pick up insider tips, see the latest tricks, and share stories of stage glory. These accomplished customers think nothing of pulling a walnut from your ear or a dove from your fanny pack. I recently bumped into Steve Cohen at Tannen's, the brilliant close-up magician who does a show called **Chamber Magic** every Friday and Saturday night at the Waldorf Astoria. Steve's live magic performance is probably the finest in America (for advance tickets go to www.chambermagic.com), and can accommodate small groups of children.

For kids who want to wear the top hat, Tannen's has some excellent beginner magic sets that offer a dozen simple tricks for around $30. Four marvelous tricks (that kids will love and can master easily) are the Spooky (the floating spirit silk), the Scotch 'N Soda (a half dollar and copper coin switch), the Magic Coloring Book (as confounding now as it was a hundred years ago), and the Svengali Deck (a hypnotic card trick). My suggestion is that you let younger children enjoy the illusion of magic as long as possible and leave the starter sets for slightly older kids.

Cool Kid's Corner

Magic happens day and night at Tannen's. Visit their website for a current listing of evening appearances at the store by an A-list of magicians from around the world. And if you really get hooked on the mysteries of magic, consider Tannen's popular Magic Camp where you could soon be mastering the Twisting Head, The Handcuff Escape, The Buzzsaw Illusion, or Girl Into Lion. Shazamm!

uptown birds

※ *Address: 522-526 Amsterdam Avenue at 85th Street*
Phone: 212-877-2473
Ideal Age Group: 3 to14
Admission: Free to browse the birds
Website: www.uptownbirds.com

We weren't allowed to have a dog or cat in the house when I was growing up (my parents were not fans of pet hair), but we did have Jolly. This orange-pink canary was only with us for a short time before succumbing to some kind of avian fever, but he was a melodic housemate and my sisters and I adored him.

At Uptown Birds, I got a chance to commune with Jolly's canary cousins along with some of the other 200 exotic birds that call the store their temporary home. Co-owner Daniel Kopulos, a soft-spoken man who grew up in a wildlife rehab family and spent two years as a zookeeper, is an animal advocate and proud that Uptown Birds sells only captive-raised birds—meaning less harm and impact on wild populations. He actually raises his spectacular birds on premises, although the sensitive breeder birds are kept in quieter quarters below the store.

Daniel also understands that his wildly colorful tropical birds—including Swainson lorikeets, yellow-bibbed lories, peach-faced lovebirds, brilliantly red eclectus parrots, African grey parrots, and rose-breasted cockatoos—are going to attract a lot of curious eyeballs. So he designed his store to showcase the spectacular plumage with three large storefront windows. Always housing a rare bird or two (look for Guyana toucanets, African pied crows and Dumont's mynahs), a parade of gapers and gawkers have stood on the sidewalk to stare since the popular store opened in late 2007.

Inside the shop, things are just as feathery. The moment you enter the front door you're facing a huge glass enclosure that houses up to ten parrots, cackling and squawking and carrying on. During birthday parties or when small school groups come in (encouraged, but you need to call ahead) children get a chance to hold these birds and hand-feed them.

Uptown Birds is not just about high flyers. They have an extensive collection of unusual reptiles and lizards, too, including blue-tongue skinks (yup, those tongues are blue), gargoyle geckos (how about that skin?), poison dart frogs (shiny, like a coin), bearded dragons, and White's "dumpy" tree frogs, as well as the ever-popular chameleons with those strange, opposable eyes. Throw in Uptown Birds' impressive collection of neon-colored tropical fish (I had my nose pressed to the tank of those clownfish, dogface puffers, and Huma Huma triggers), and you can understand why I call this the best, totally free menagerie in the entire city.

Cool Kid's Corner

Sometimes when Guyana toucanets sunbathe in Uptown Birds' display windows, they lie on the ground, head tilted, with wings spread wide open. More than once, outraged passersby have called the ASPCA to report dead birds and store negligence. Nope, those are just happy toucs taking a nap!

west side kids

✳ *Address: 498 Amsterdam at 84th Street*
Phone: 212-496-7282
Ideal Age Group: 2 to 8
Admission: Free

According to local lore, Alice Bergman, owner of the superb West Side Kids toy store, stopped selling Beanie Babies when she saw an adult collector aggressively snatch a popular Beanie from the hands of a toddler. That's real child advocacy, folks.

Stories like these are why West Side Kids gets my vote as the best toy store in the city. Kids come first here, not to mention that this independent, family-owned business has been selling an extraordinary selection of retro playthings, thoughtfully selected toys, books and games for more than 25 years.

Alice's daughter, Leslie, is the driving force at the store now, bringing with her a degree in child development and a strong sense of the right games for enhancing creative play and building developmental skills. In the course of five minutes, I watched Leslie explain the rules of a new board game to a mother buying a birthday gift, and then tell a little girl about a beautiful storybook and why she might like it.

The fact is that Alice and Leslie handpick, hand play, personally read and intimately know every game, gift, gadget, picture book, puzzle, science experiment and crafts project in the place, and it's an education just stepping through the door. Lots of people do. Some just to say hello (that happens when you're in the same neighborhood for a quarter century and care about the community's kids), others to pet the store dogs, Joey and Jake, but most to buy a gift for someone under ten in a store where they know they'll get great personal attention . . . plus free gift-wrapping!

Something else you should know about West Side Kids is that they carry almost no electronics—a courageous choice by the Bergmans in a world where mainstream toy stores survive on Wii's, Playstations, and video games. Instead, you'll find classics like Tinker Toys, Lincoln Logs, Sand Art, and Magic Garden, as well as new favorites—sturdy Kettler trikes, Bruder trucks, award-winning Gymini activity environments, an extensive Kumon Books section (the Japanese system for fast, fun learning) and the popular Zingo game (Bingo with a zing). There's a big bubble selection, handcrafted wooden train sets, cool spy night goggles and wrist gadgets, sensational costumes for dress-up, a music section with kazoos, rattles, tambourines and drums, plus balsa-wood gliders, stickers galore, and hacky-sacks. Most of the store's merchandise is arranged thematically and, as Leslie is proud to point out, it's chosen for play value, non-gender specific qualities, and multi-cultural appeal. And since we all care more than ever about how and where our toys are made, West Side Kids carries loads of eco-safe and non-toxic playthings.

Cool Kid's Corner

When you're done exploring at West Side Kids, walk a block to the Children's Museum of Manhattan (212 West 83rd Street; 212-721-1234; www.cmom.org), where it's bursting with drop-in, non-stop play action on five fantastic floors. You can come for a performance or interactive program, too, because lots of times they let you be the star. Are you ready?

winnie-the-pooh
and friends

❊ *Address: New York Public Library, The Children's*
Center at 42nd Street and 5th Avenue
Phone: 212-621-0205
Ideal Age Group: 3 to 14
Admission: Free
Website: www.nypl.org/branch/central/dlc/dch/pooh

I first discovered the reassuring sweetness of the Winnie-the-Pooh books during a rough patch in my early thirties. My life had become anxiety filled and difficult, and I was feeling small and frightened. Quite by accident, I stumbled upon A. A. Milne's 1920s children's classics, and read myself to sleep with Pooh and his friends for months. The Bear of Very Little Brain made me smile, and Piglet's tiny vulnerability made me feel my own. I could sympathize with Eeyore's gloominess because I was feeling the same way, while I longed for Tigger's bounciness and Kanga's mothering. Spending time in the calming rhythms of the Hundred Acre Wood was healing, and I'm grateful for it.

What many children today don't realize is that the hero of the series, Christopher Robin, was the actual son of A. A. Milne, and that his cherished stuffed animal family was quite real. What's even more amazing is that five of Christopher Milne's original toy companions (including Pooh) left England in 1947 and now live permanently here in New York at the New York Public Library's Children's Center—a bright new home created for the clan of the Pooh bear in the spring of 2009.

You can't help but feel awed and excited as you approach the famous faces of Tigger, Kanga, Eeyore, and Piglet, sitting silently in a climate-controlled glass case (no Rabbit or Owl—

they must have stayed behind in England). But it's the sight of Pooh sitting nobly in the center that makes your heart skip a beat. This is not the Disney animation Pooh, not a cheap stuffed imitation Pooh, not a painted lunchbox Pooh, but the original Edward Bear who went "bump, bump, bump" down the stairs behind Christopher Robin. Oh, what I'd give to cuddle that furry fellow for just a minute or two.

Bring your own copy of the Pooh tales when you come to visit. As you look down upon Christopher Robin's original best friends, remember sweet passages like this one—an exchange between the gentle bear and Piglet that has always stayed with me:

Piglet sidled up to Pooh from behind.

"Pooh," he whispered.

"Yes, Piglet."

"Nothing," said Piglet, taking Pooh's paw. "I just wanted to be sure of you."

Be sure to sign Pooh's guest book, along with thousands of other children and adult fans from around the world who have already sworn their devotion.

Cool Kid's Corner

Look closely and you'll see that Christopher Robin loved his plush pals well—Piglet's skin has been hugged right down to the raw fabric, Kanga's neck has been squeezed so hard it has required several surgeries, and the downcast Eeyore wears more than one patch to repair his hide. In fact, if you've got really good eyes you'll notice a very fine netting over Eeyore's body applied by museum curators trying to protect the weary gray donkey. The other characters get the same first class treatment.

✳20 more great places to take kids

(Just for the fun of it!)

baseball center of NYC

❊ *Address: 202 West 74th Street between Broadway and Amsterdam*

Phone: 212-362-0344

Ideal Age Group: 6 to 14

Admission: $50 for half hour, up to 5 kids; $80 for one hour

Website: www.thebaseballcenternyc.com

Now that the likes of the Red Sox and Rays are snagging division championships, we'll have to work harder preparing the next generation of hometown heroes. And when it comes to creating a future crop of Derek Jeters and Carlos Beltrans, the Baseball Center NYC hits a towering home run. The best indoor facility in the city, this high-tech baseball training center offers baseball and softball enthusiasts a year-round place to practice the fine art of hitting, pitching, base running and fielding. Kids can get professional instruction here, and the center throws an excellent birthday party, too, that can include favors like stadium cups, batting helmets, and personalized baseball bats. But I like the idea of simply taking two of your favorite sluggers down to the cages (they've got four batting cages with state-of-the-art pitching machines) and letting them hit up to 600 balls in the span of an hour. The Baseball Center isn't cheap, but your kids will be talking about the way they connected with that 70-mph fastball for months. And there's always the chance of a brush with a pro-slugger— Paul Loduca, Jorge Posada, David Ortiz, Mariano Rivera, even Olympic softball star Jennie Finch have stopped by the center in the past.

biking the hudson river greenway

❊ *Address: Battery Park to 178th Street*
Ideal Age Group: 5 to 14
Admission: Free (Bike Rentals at 44th Street and the
Hudson River)

It was my blue Schwinn Stingray with the banana seat, the two-foot sissy bar, and the stick shift that launched my obsession with biking. My first bike was also my first foray into freedom. But where does a Manhattan kid find a place to ride safely and close to home? The spectacular Hudson River Greenway, opening miles of riverfront to little bikers and tikers, is the answer. This landscaped esplanade runs from Battery Park to the northern tip of the island. Smooth, paved paths keep children safely away from motorized traffic as they pass notable sights like enormous ocean liners, miniature golf courses, helicopter pads, kayak boathouses, fishing coves, new water parks, the giant green bottle at the 96th Street Pier, and the massive *Intrepid* aircraft carrier (page 49). If your child can handle the distance, take the path to The Little Red Lighthouse, under the George Washington Bridge. The Urban Park Rangers offer a tour of the light from spring through fall (212-304-2365), which includes a reading of the children's classic, *The Little Red Lighthouse and the Great Grey Bridge*, which made the landmark so famous.

bowlmor lanes

❊ *Address: 110 University Place between 12th and 13th Streets*

Phone: 212-255-8188

Ideal Age Group: 6 to 14

Admission: $10.95 per person per game / $6.50 for shoes (no children after 5 P.M.)

Website: www.bowlmor.com

Gone are the days of boring white pins and plain black balls. At Bowlmor Lanes the satisfying sound of heavy orbs crashing against ten sitting ducks is accompanied by techno-color innovations—neon green, yellow, orange, and red pins, balls of every hue (and lightweight ones for little people), plus a powerful sound system. Bowlmor's stylish interior has brought out a new breed of bowler—young and hip. Kids love the high decibel DJ music, the effortless automatic scoring, the 12-foot video screens at the end of every lane, the outrageously delicious chicken fingers, the snazzy shoes, and the high probability of spotting a famous bowler (celebs with children are plentiful in this downtown neighborhood). In fact, Bowlmor keeps dozens of autographed pins in the display cases from recent guests like singers Alicia Keys, Usher, and Lenny Kravitz, actors Matt Damon, Cameron Diaz, and Ashley Olsen, plus comedian Conan O'Brien and so many others. Bowling bashes are good for birthdays, too, and at Bowlmor they throw a series of strikes when it comes to children's parties.

chinatown ice cream factory

* *Address: 65 Bayard Street between Mott and Elizabeth Streets*
  Phone: 212-608-4170
  Ideal Age Group: 2 to 14
  Admission: $3.75 per hearty scoop in a cone
  Website: www.chinatownicecreamfactory.com

Many a cranky kid has been mollified with ice cream, and if you're going to use this sweet magic as either bribe or reward, you might as well choose the best. More than one emphatic parent told me that the freshest, creamiest, most irresistible ice cream in New York is served up at the Chinatown Ice Cream Factory (CICF). Run by local businessman Philip Seid and his family for three decades, it is now daughter Christina Seid who presides over the creation of more than 40 flavors of ice cream and sorbet on premises from natural ingredients. The Asian specialties—like ginger, black sesame, mango, green tea, taro, and red bean—are buttery and exotic, but Philip tells me the current favorites among aficionados are lychee, Oreo cookie, coconut fudge, and pineapple. I was instantly hooked on the double scoop of almond cookie and banana—the most intensely flavored ice creams I've ever tasted. There is no atmosphere here, but that's not the point—it's about freakin' awesome ice cream, all of which you can sample on a little spoon before you buy. If your children are already talking about their next scoops five minutes after you've left the store, go back for a hand-packed quart of their favorite flavor and bring it home. You might consider buying a CICF t-shirt, too—kids adore that image of the baby green dragon enjoying his own scoop.

city treehouse

❋ *Address: 129 A West 20th Street, between 6th and 7th Avenues*

Phone: 212-255-2050

Ideal Age: 18 months to 8

Admission: Pay-as-you go, with $50 annual membership, then as little as $12.50 per visit; first visit free

Website: www.citytreehouse.com

The Chelsea district has become increasingly family friendly in recent years, and City Treehouse is making its amiable contribution. This well-designed, 4300-square-foot indoor play center has two distinguishing features—a large water play area and an impressive treehouse. The "Splash" area is built around a shallow stream table with plenty of water jets, sprinklers, fountains, and hoses. A generous assortment of water toys—boats, measuring cups, pouring pitchers, as well as plastic hippos, sea turtles, balls, and bugs—keep kids engaged. Colorful waterproof smocks are available along with paper towels and blow dryers if splashing becomes frenzied. Older kids are drawn to the massive tree, with its hollow hideout inside the trunk and a metal slide extending along its side. They dash around the tree base, scoot up the circular stairs covered with a synthetic grass surface to an upper level, then shoot down the stainless steel slide, only to repeat the loop endlessly. City Treehouse was created by Sydney Price, a mother of twin girls who liked the idea of an imaginative play and learning center and saw a neighborhood need. Having the presence of a knowing mom is a definite plus; the play space is dotted with bins marked "Yuck Buckets"— receptacles for objects that are sneezed on, coughed over, or otherwise contaminated, and ready for sanitizing. That's mom protection at its finest.

dieu donné

❊ *Address: 315 West 36th Street between 8th and
9th Avenues*
Phone: 212-226-0573
Admission: Call about family papermaking workshops and
group birthday party packages
Ideal Age Group: 7 to 12
Website: www.dieudonne.org

Why do all kids love papermaking? It's wet and messy and fun.
And the best way for children to learn how to turn pulp into
paper is to take a lesson from the folks who've been doing it
for more than 30 years at Dieu Donné. While there are no
walk-in classes, this might be the best educational birthday
party idea or family outing in New York. First, you'll see the
mill's skilled artists make the raw material by cutting,
shredding and beating pieces of cotton and linen in water to
create a soupy pulp. Then you get to play in this goop. Using
basic tools—a mould, a deckle, and a felt—you shake out and
form your own paper sheets. Finally, you throw on all sorts of
squirtable colors, collage materials, glitter, even leaves and
flowers, to decorate your creation. When I went, I made a
small blue sheet with the initials "A.I." squirted on top in
yellow, which I thought was cool. Then I noticed an 11-year-
old next to me who had taken a wad of semidried pulp and
squeezed it into a kind of paper baseball. Wish I'd thought
of that.

FAO schwarz

Address: 767 Fifth Avenue at 58th Street
Phone: 212-644-9400
Ideal Age Group: 2 to 12
Admission: Free
Website: www.fao.com

There's probably no single name in New York more strongly associated with children than FAO Schwarz. This world famous toy store began catering to the imaginations of kids in 1862, and it's still rocking today. Say hello to the 12-foot teddy bear sitting out front, take a photo with the real-life toy soldier guarding the entrance door, then step into this magnificent 50,000-square-foot playroom. On your left, a life-sized stuffed giraffe and baby elephant; on your right, a two-story tree house; straight ahead, an ice cream parlor and candy land; in the back, acres of Barbies, wind-up toys, board games, and magic tricks; upstairs, adoptable Nursery Newborns and the enormous Dance-On Piano with professional performances every 15 minutes (join them and tap out a tune). More? How about the only dedicated Harry Potter Shop in the country, a plush den showing constant kids' movies, princes and princesses walking the floor, video games, actions figures, radio-controlled racers, and electric Ferraris and Jeeps that give kids a license to drive. And if all this isn't enough, FAO is absolutely, positively the stuffed animal capital of the world. Cuddling is allowed. Sucking thumb while cuddling is a little weird.

firestore and NY911

Address: 17 Greenwich Avenue between Christopher and West 10th Street
Phone: 212-226-3142
Ideal Age: 3 to 12
Admission: Free to browse
Website: www.nyfirestore.com

Located next to Ladder Company 20 in SoHo for 15 years, this little shop carrying all things related to firefighters became a virtual shrine to New York's Bravest after September 11, 2001. Now in larger digs across town in Greenwich Village, the Firestore incorporates the NY911 store (paying tribute to New York's Finest). But it's still the place where firefighters from around the world come for something, anything NYFDish, so you're likely to rub shoulders with *pompiers* from Paris and *bomberos* from Barcelona. Fire-themed gifts for adults include new and recycled firemen's coats, but it's the kids' gear that's really hot (sorry). Store owners Noam and Annie Freedman carry plenty for firefighter wannabes, including black plastic helmets, fire bears, firefighter pajamas, black-and-yellow firefighter raincoats that look regulation issue, and the most extensive collection of FDNY official patch and firehouse patch designs available on the planet. If you like the traditional T-shirt with FDNY on the front, and KEEP BACK 200 FT. on the flip side, they have them in sizes for the whole family. The **NY911** police store carries everything from authentic NYPD tees and detective caps to cool stuff for fans of the FBI, the DEA, and Special Ops. If you're thinking this is a wonderful store to both meet and honor our city's greatest heroes, you'd be right.

forbes magazine galleries

❊ *Address: 62 Fifth Avenue at 12th Street*
Phone: 212-206-5548
Ideal Age Group: 5 to 12
Admission: Free
Website: www.forbesgalleries.com

I have a friend in his seventies who plays adult war games with toy soldiers every Thursday night—he calls it his greatest passion and an extension of an obsession that he has had with tin miniatures since he was a child. Clearly, this obsession was shared by Malcolm Forbes, the consummate capitalist and famous publisher who collected toys all his life and ultimately packed many of them into the dignified Forbes Magazine Galleries. For young children accustomed to today's touch-it-all museum experience, the Forbes toy room might prove a bit too refined and subdued. But the elaborate scenes behind the display windows are so meticulously presented, and the sheer numbers of rusting warships and tiny tin cowboys so striking, that children get deliciously lost in their imaginations. Included in the collection is the only *Lusitania* model manu-factured by famous toy ship builder Marklin, as well as 12,000 of the more than 100,000 Civil War soldiers, medieval knights, Plains Indians, GIs, and Aztecs contained in the Forbes collection. Also displayed are a number of other priceless items like presidential letters, Abe Lincoln's stovepipe hat, and inventor Charles Darrow's original hand-painted Monopoly game board. Some of these exotic collectibles are less interesting to young children, but I did notice one ten-year-old standing before Honest Abe's black hat for more than five minutes, obviously in awe.

high line park

※ *Address: Gansevoort Street to 34th Street on Manhattan's far West Side*

Phone: 212-206-9922

Ideal Age: 2 to 14

Admission: Free

Website: www.thehighline.org

The new High Line Park puts kids above trucks and traffic and is a little like walking on air. When fully completed it will be a one-and-a-half-mile strip of peaceful gardens and sitting areas weaving through 22 West Side blocks at a height of 18 to 30 feet. Renewal of the old, abandoned elevated railways began in 2006 and the first section from Gansevoort Street to 20th Street was opened in 2009. It includes foot-cooling water features, dedicated children's play areas, viewing platforms, ample sundecks, and gathering nooks for performances and art exhibitions. The first day it opened it was a magnet for families looking for a safe, beautiful place to hang out with their children without having to worry about speeding cars or terror cyclists. Tranquil and green, the High Line brilliantly recaptures an industrial steel-and-concrete icon of the city and turns it into a recreational jewel. Your kids are going to love every elevated minute. For an added treat, leave the High Line promenade at Pier 62 near 23rd Street and make your way to the new **Chelsea Carousel**, opening in early 2010. With 33 wooden characters native to the region—including a black bear, peregrine falcon, harbor seal, coyote, white tail deer, rabbit, and skunk—plus a fantasy unicorn and a wheelchair accessible oyster chariot, this merry-go-round is going to light up a lot of young faces.

homer's world famous malt shop

❋ *Address: 487 Amsterdam Avenue between 83rd and 84th Streets*
Phone: 212-496-0777
Ideal Age: 4 to 10
Admission: Menu items start at $2.50 for a hot dog
Website: www.homersworldfamous.com

Let's eat. I'll have a grilled cheese sandwich, a root beer float, and a Rice Krispie treat for dessert. You have the chicken tenders, a milkshake, and a brownie. We'll watch Boomerang at the table in front of the big plasma TV. And you can play classic video games like Donkey Kong or Pac-Man while we wait for our food. Sound good? Sounds like Homer's, the very popular eatery on the Upper West Side that specializes in kid food, kid TV, and kid fun from late morning until late afternoon. And in a city where eating out with several children can be prohibitively expensive, Homer's saves the day. The menu here is made for a little person's palate—and your wallet—with standards like peanut butter and jelly, pigs-in-a-blanket, fried mozzarella sticks, frosty fountain drinks, and locally-made ice cream with a dozen favorite toppings. At Homer's, you can take the whole brood out for lunch with enough money left to come back tomorrow. And, trust me, with good eats plus video bowling, toy cranes, and air hockey, returning is *exactly* what your kids will want to do.

jamaica bay wildlife refuge

❊ *Address: Gateway National Park, Cross Bay Boulevard, Queens*

Phone: 718-354-4606

Ideal Age: 6 to 14

Admission: Free

Website: www.nps.gov/gate

Look, up in the sky, it's a bird, it's a plane, it's . . . another bird. At this incredibly beautiful refuge it's all about ospreys, herons, egrets, hawks, ducks, geese, barn owls, warblers, woodcocks, and hundreds of other species of wild, flying things. Part of the Gateway National Recreation Area, this is one of the largest bird sanctuaries in the northeast (more than 9,000 acres), situated on a major migratory flyway. Which means in spring and fall this is the place to see seasonal bird migrations (more than 300 species have been observed). Serious bird watchers flock here, and since birding requires patience and "the quiet voice," it's not right for every child. But if physical and vocal restraint are possible for your children, then don't miss the pristine salt marshes, fields, woods, and ponds that make up this sanctuary—located within city limits and easily accessible by the "A" train. Along with the song and shorebirds, children love to spot butterflies, reptiles (look for the "terrapin nesting path"), amphibians, and small mammals along the trails. This is a winning day trip for the entire family. Wear waterproof shoes and bring binoculars.

karma kids yoga

✳ *Address: 104 West 14th Street near 6th Avenue, 2nd floor*

Phone: 646-638-1444

Ideal Age: 3 to 12

Admission: $25 Drop-In Class; 10-Class Package from $220

Website: www.karmakidsyoga.com

Take your favorite yoga class, add a purple-painted backdrop, playful instructors, and a heaping helping of songs, art, stories, games, and laughs, and you'll know what to expect at Karma Kids Yoga. Here, your standard Down Dog, Tree, and Warrior poses are cleverly transformed into more animated movements like Balloon Belly, Jelly Legs, Grasshopper, Making Cake, and Roller Coaster pose. The traditional Cat and Cow postures are accompanied by "meows" and "moos," while hissing happens in Cobra pose. This children-only studio (with classes in Brooklyn, too) has perfected a method for making yoga engaging and fun for kids, while stretching and strengthening their developing bodies. My favorite Karma creation is "toga," where children practice balancing while picking up colored pom-poms with their toes and dropping them into wicker baskets. Another stimulating place for physical expression is **Steps on Broadway** (2121 Broadway at 74th Street; 212-874-2410; www.stepsnyc.com), where kids can take hip-hop, ballet, jazz, tap, and musical theater classes, while surrounded by serious adult dancers and taught by the professional dancers they aspire to become.

national track & field hall of fame

❊ *Address: 216 Fort Washington Avenue at West 168th Street*
Phone: 212-923-1803
Ideal Age: 7 to 14
Admission: $5 per person
Website: www. ny.milesplit.us/pages/Hall-of-Fame

Quick, what's America's #1 high school sport? No, it's not football. Not baseball or basketball either. It's track and field, with 1.35 million athletes involved on the high school level and more than five million boys and girls participating overall. Of course, a sport this popular needs its own Hall of Fame, and this one opened in 2004 at The Armory on 168th Street—currently the busiest indoor track and field center in the country. There's no shortage of terrific memorabilia here, like Carl Lewis's long jump shoes from the 1996 Olympics, the bodysuit worn by since disgraced Marion Jones in the Sydney Games, Steve Prefontaine's University of Oregon singlet and shorts, championship vaulting poles, javelins, even a leather shot put from 1885. In the second floor hallway you'll find a sixty-yard sprint track for event day warm-ups (also used by speedy visitors to outrun pesky siblings). But the real adrenaline rush is on the third and fourth floors, where kids get a jaw-dropping view of The Armory's indoor track—the fastest in the world (that's not bluster, it's based on winning times). Visit during the track and field season (December through March) to see history measured in seconds on The Armory's famed oval.

new york city fire museum

* *Address: 278 Spring Street between Hudson and Varick Streets*
Phone: 212-691-1303
Ideal Age Group: 4 to 8
Admission: $5 adults / $1 children (suggested)
Website: www.nycfiremuseum.org

Organized firefighting in this city began with the men of the Rattle Watch, a sharp-eyed and, apparently, sharp-nosed team that prowled our streets at night looking for fires, spinning loud rattles to alert residents if they sniffed a blaze. Dedicated junior firefighters will love this overflowing museum for fire facts like that one and much more. Situated in a pristine former firehouse, this turn-of-the-century, three-story building has rare Colonial-era leather fire buckets, torch lights, axes, alarm boxes, ornate hose nozzles, goose-neck pumpers, and a slightly macabre, stuffed firehouse dog named Chief that was a favorite of his engine company in the 1940s. They also have plenty of boots, jackets, helmets and firefighter air packs for you to try on.

If you need a real life encore, your neighborhood firehouse is often very kid-friendly. If the firefighters aren't racing to a scene, and you don't stay too long, you can usually drop by for a tour. Inside are the rolling red monsters with awesome tires the height of second-graders and water hoses as thick as boa constrictors. Know why most of the firefighters leave their shoes untied or wear slip-on shoes? So they can kick them off fast when the alarm sounds and jump into a pair of those big boots lined up against the walls.

next level learning

※ *Address: 850 7th Avenue between 54th and 55th Streets*
Phone: 212-957-9100
Ideal Age: 6 to 14
Admission: Check website for current tutoring rates
Website: www.nyclearn.com

Parents everywhere want their children to get a good education. In New York City, academic competition is heightened by a highly selective admissions process to the best schools, along with increasing pressure to perform on standardized tests. As a result, more and more parents are seeking outside tutoring services as a way to help their kids stay ahead. You need look no further than Next Level Learning, a midtown center that specializes in a one-on-one, personalized approach. Next Level's director, Valerie Fitzhugh, has an almost preternatural ability to connect with kids, an extraordinary gift that she seems to have conveyed to her competent staff of top-tier educators. Valerie believes that all kids are curious, smart, creative and capable. They freak out and fall behind in school when they get intimidated by new concepts, lose confidence, or start to believe they are less intelligent than other kids. At Next Level, success is achieved by creating a caring relationship with each student that allows him or her to relax, become engaged, and have fun learning again. Fast progress is the result. I have seen the Next Level team in action and it's impressive. Kids are smiling and joking with tutors, tutors are high-fiving and encouraging kids, ideas are flying, confidence is building, and learning is happening. It's a playful, yet powerful scene. It doesn't hurt that Next Level Learning has the lowest rates for one-on-one tutoring in the city, so families are ensured an excellent value in these tight economic times.

pier 84 splash fountain

❊ *Address: West 44th Street at the Hudson River*

Ideal Age: 3 to 10

Admission: Free

new york's 50 best places to take children

The parks department calls it a "programmed interactive fountain," but kids just call it wet, wild, and hilarious fun. It lies in wait at the foot of Pier 84—now the largest public pier park along the Hudson with 98,000 square feet of gardens, lawns, water play areas, and river viewing docks. What I love about this quirky fountain is the way it engages every child who passes by with its unpredictable splash dance. Squirt holes are arranged within a series of concentric circles about 40 feet in diameter and lie flush with the pink granite sidewalk—until they don't. Suddenly, jets of water rise up as high as 8 feet in the air and disappear just as quickly. Children toss their shoes to the side, roll up their jeans, and try to time the waterspout intervals to avoid a drenching. I watched a group of European kids playing a cool game, dashing around the concentric maze at high speed, spiraling into the center as they dodged the erratic water jets. Folks sitting at the adjacent outdoor café at P. D. O'Hurley's laughed and applauded, while the next group of kids got in line. On sunny days, three seasons of the year, this is a perfect place to stop and play as you make your way between the *Intrepid* (page 49) and the nearby **New York Waterway Sightseeing Cruises** (page 81). Splash Fountain bonus: Watching adults attempt the mad dash, resulting in some very humorous and squishy results.

puppetworks

❄ *Address: 338 6th Avenue at 4th Street,*
Brooklyn
Phone: 718-965-3391
Ideal Age: 3 to 8
Admission: $8 adults / $7 children
Website: www.puppetworks.org

Located on the corner of a residential block of brownstones in Park Slope, PuppetWorks lacks a glittery commercial façade, but don't let the humble storefront throw you. There's magic waiting behind the front door, which opens to eager kids a half hour before the start of each show. The best seats in the house are up close—grab a spot on one of the big red floor mats near the stage (the equivalent of orchestra seating).

While you're waiting for the lights to go down, see if you can spot Hansel, Gretel, the Witch, and at least a hundred other puppets from classic children's stories festooning the turquoise walls (their Pinocchio puppet has been in the company's lineage since 1938, when it was part of the Suzari Marionettes that toured school groups in Brooklyn). PuppetWorks' marvelous performances are almost a rite of passage for children in this pleasant neighborhood. The reasons why are evident the moment the curtain rises and talented puppeteers work the strings and animate the handmade figures. When the curtain falls, the fun continues as one of the performers demonstrates the workings of a marionette to a wide-eyed audience. One seven-year-old named Aaron spoke for a gaggle of devoted young fans at a recent performance when he reported that "PuppetWorks is my favorite puppet theater."

south street seaport buskers

✳ *Address: 12 Fulton Street*
Phone: 212-748-8786
Ideal Age Group: 2 to 14
Admission: Free to marketplace / Fees vary for museums and historic ships
Website: www.southstreetseaportmuseum.org

The South Street Seaport is 12 square blocks of restored nineteenth-century buildings dating back to the 1600s that attract more than ten million visitors a year. Children are drawn to the Seaport's historic tall ships like the *Peking*—a 347-foot, four-masted giant that's the second-largest sailing ship in the world, as well as the century-old schooner, *Pioneer*, where kids can help raise the sails or even take the helm (operates seasonally). But I think the single most appealing children's attraction at the Seaport is the incredible concentration of buskers, or street performers. From May through October, the Seaport encourages street artists to entertain along the cobblestone pedestrian walkways (they actually hold auditions in April), and these multi-talented artists are everywhere. What results is an amazingly vibrant carnival, a street circus, a colorful world of jugglers, magicians, mimes, musicians, puppeteers, and balloon sculptors. And all this entertainment is free. One summer Sunday I listened to a guitarist play a medley of Neil Young tunes, watched a magician struggle to rip himself free of a straitjacket in under two minutes, stood with mouth agape as an acrobat juggled carving knives, and heard a comedian do 20 minutes of G-rated material that had adults howling along with their kids. Besides that, street performance is a dying art that gives the city soul—buskers are cool.

wollman rink

※ *Address: Mid-Central Park at 63rd Street*
Phone: 212-439-6900
Ideal Age Group: 5 to 14
Admission: $10 adult, $5.25 children, $6 skate rental
(from October through March)
Website: www.wollmanskatingrink.com

The Rockefeller Center Rink is the stuff of legend, and the new winter rink in Bryant Park is free, but if you want an unforgettable New York experience, you've got to take the kids ice-skating in Central Park. The best place to do that is at the Wollman Rink where there is lots of open sky overhead, trees all around, and the stately hotels and residences of Central Park South casting afternoon shadows over the landscape. This skyline view is so breathtaking, not to mention famous, that even children stop their lazy loops to look up and stare. It's marvelous on winter evenings, too, when the glittering lights of the surrounding buildings add to the fantasy feeling. True skating enthusiasts can sign up for a youth ice hockey league and skating school that share the ice in the heavy sweater days of fall and winter. There is picturesque public skating at **Kate Wollman Rink** in Brooklyn's Prospect Park, too (www.prospectpark.org), with good hot chocolate in the winter and an ample 26,600 square feet of groomed ice where you can carve your finest figure eights.

six day trips for foolproof fun

If your time in New York is limited, you'll want to make the most of every day. I've compiled these six sure-to-please day trips so you can plan your visit with kids more easily and maximize your fun. They're grouped by geography and for diversity of experience, but all ensure a great outing.

I've tried to consider variables like seasons (since playgrounds are less appealing in the city winds of winter) and overall cost (because too many museum fees tend to make adults crankier than the kids). Keep in mind that if you plan to visit up to two locations, you'll need to allow a few hours. If you're going to try to squeeze in three or more, you'll need to break for lunch and plan to spend a full day.

To ensure optimal happiness for your entire entourage, bring along these minimal supplies: a map or two, bottled water or juice, a few snacks, and comfortable shoes. And don't forget your MetroCard!

1. Upper East Side

This trip takes advantage of some ultra-kid-friendly locales in Central Park, and adds a few new hot spots to the mix, along with some old favorites.

Sony Wonder Technology Lab (page 97)
550 Madison Avenue at East 56th Street

Central Park Zoo (page 35)
Central Park at East 64th Street

Alice in Wonderland Sculpture (page 15)
Central Park at Fifth Avenue and East 74th Street

Kerbs Conservatory Water Sailboats (page 51)
Central Park at East 74th Street near Fifth Avenue

New York Doll Hospital (page 75)
787 Lexington Avenue between East 61st and East 62nd Streets

2. Upper West Side

Outside, inside, upside down . . . this tour combines puppets, dinosaur bones, hippopotami, a tour of the universe, and the chance to buy some really cool yo-yos.

Swedish Marionette Theater (page 99)
Central Park at West 81st Street

Rose Center for Earth and Space (page 93)
Central Park West at West 81st Street

American Museum of Natural History (page 21)
Central Park West at West 79th Street

West Side Kids (page 109)
498 Amsterdam Avenue at 84th Street

Hippo Playground (page 47)
Riverside Drive at West 91st Street

3. Midtown Day Trip #1

Start off at skyscraper central and then head west. Be sure to check the Manhattan bus map before you travel over to the Hudson. The Westbound M50 bus is especially convenient for this trip—hop on at 6th Avenue until the bus turns south down 12th Avenue, and get out at 46th Street; for the return trip, hop back on the M50 bus on 12th Avenue and head east again.

FDNY Fire Zone (page 45)
34 West 51st Street between 5th and 6th Avenues

Mars 2112 (page 63)
1633 Broadway at West 51st Street

Intrepid **Sea-Air-Space Museum (page 49)**
Pier 86, West 46th Street on the Hudson River

4. Midtown Day Trip #2

Today, jaws are going to drop and eyes will open wide and they'll likely stay that way until dinnertime.

Madame Tussauds New York (page 59)
234 West 42nd Street between 7th and 8th Avenues

Ripley's Believe It or Not! (page 87)
234 West 42nd Street between 7th and 8th Avenues

Tannen's Magic (page 105)
45 West 34th Street between 5th and 6th Avenues

5. Downtown

What could be better than fooling with Flubber and filling up on fresh Zen Butter ice cream? That depends on what else you want to do—check out the awesomest playground, see amazing sword-juggling acrobats, or visit the coolest sports museum. Ever.

Children's Museum of the Arts (page 39)
182 Lafayette Street between Broome and Grand Streets

Chinatown Ice Cream Factory (page 117)
65 Bayard Street between Elizabeth and Mott Streets

Rockefeller Playground (Option 1): After your ice cream break, you can walk just a few blocks south to Worth Street and catch the Westbound M22 bus to Rockefeller Playground (page 89; Vesey Street on the Hudson River).

South Street Seaport Buskers (Option 2): Or, if you're wearing your walking shoes with a good city map in hand, and the kids have their sneakers on and the energy, head down to see the South Street Seaport Buskers (page 132; 12 Fulton Street).

6. Brooklyn

There are so many places to go in this family friendly borough, it's hard to know where best to launch the day. You can start out at the New York Transit Museum, then take the bus or subway to the Brooklyn Children's Museum. Don't forget Kate Wollman Rink (page 133) in the winter or many wonderful playgrounds, fields, nature trails, the zoo, and the Carousel in Prospect Park (page 33). And if you're on the western edge of the Park, be sure to stop at the Harmony/9th Street Playground (page 90), or swing by Park Slope's nearby PuppetWorks (page 131) to catch a weekend performance. Make sure to pick up bus and subway maps at the transit museum and keep them handy!

New York Transit Museum (page 79)
Boerum Place and Schermerhorn Street, Brooklyn Heights

Brooklyn Children's Museum (page 31)
145 Brooklyn Avenue at St. Mark's Avenue, Brooklyn

Prospect Park Carousel (page 33)
East side of Prospect Park at Ocean Avenue (near Prospect Park Q/B and Franklin Avenue shuttle subway stops)

✳index

(by neighborhood)

neighborhood index

manhattan: south of canal street (tribeca/chinatown)

canal street to 14th street (soho/village)

14th street to 34th street (chelsea/flatiron/gramercy)

34th street to 59th street (midtown)

59th street to 92nd street (upper east side)

59th street to 92nd street (upper west side)

central park

above 125th street (inwood/washington heights)

bronx

brooklyn

queens

new jersey

new york's 50 best places to take children

the best children's web sources for new york city

In New York City, it's impossible for a kid to be bored. There is just so much to do and the fantastic attractions change daily. Here are some excellent online sources for updated information on events, parades, exhibitions, activities, performances and appearances of interest for families with children. Be sure to check them frequently, as cool things to do with kids pop up minute-by-minute.

- **Time Out New York Kids at www.timeoutnykids.com**
  The first place I look for up-to-the minute things to do with young ones and they always have a current list of the best kid-friendly restaurants.
- **New York Magazine online at www.nymag.com/family/kids**
  New Yorkers rely on the print magazine for reliable entertainment ideas and the online counterpart for kids is always a solid source for great attractions.
- **Parent Zone at www.parentzone.com/usa/new-york/new-york**
  The Family Fun page is a good resource for unexpected, offbeat attractions that kids love.
- **NY Metro Parents at www.parentsknow.com**
  Chock full of useful information for New York City parents. I'm a fan of their Parent's Community blog.
- **ParentGuide at www.parentguidenews.com**
  I always find something current and rewarding to do at their Calendar of Events page.
- **New York Convention & Visitor's Bureau at www.nycvisit.com**
  You have to drill down a bit to get to the good stuff here, but occasionally this website has an unexpected gem for families traveling to NYC.
- **About.com at www.gonyc.about.com**
  The New York City with Kids link offers a wellspring of ideas.